The Magnificent Bears of North America

The Magnificent Bears of North America ... and Where to Find Them

A "WHERE TO EASILY FIND 'EM" BOOK
by Keith Scott — "The Bear Man"

HANCOCK HOUSE
WHERE TO EASILY FIND 'EM SERIES

Observing wild birds and mammals has become North America's most popular sport. The Hancock House WHERE TO EASILY FIND 'EM SERIES of books is designed to present an easy-to-follow guide to understanding species behavior, to enable the reader to predict the correct habitat and time for best observation and also to provide maps to some specific locations.

Other Works by Keith Scott:
Don't Always Blame the Bear
Hiking in Bear Country
My Adventures With Bears
Bears Have their Own Language
Fish Creek and Salmon Glacier
I Should've Made The Globetrotters
The Great Bears of Hyder, Alaska, & Stewart, B.C.

Available on Video:
Hiking in Moose and Bear Country
First Hike Alone
My Son and I Camping
Hike to the Top
New Brunswick: The Picture Province

The Magnificent Bears of North America

... and Where to Find Them

Keith Scott
"The Bear Man"

hancock
house

ISBN 0-88839-494-2
Copyright © 2001 Scott, Keith Vincent

Cataloging in Publication Data
Scott, Keith, 1936–
The magnificent bears of North America, and where to find them

Includes index.
ISBN 0-88839-494-2

1. Bears—North America. I. Title.
QL737.C27S363 2001   599.78'097   C2001-910329-8

Production and cover design: Melanie Clark and Gayle Shulhan
Front cover photograph: Keith Scott
Back cover photographs: Keith Scott

We acknowledge the financial support of the Government of Canada through the Book Publishing Industry Development Program for our publishing activities.

Published simultaneously in Canada and the United States by

HANCOCK HOUSE PUBLISHERS LTD.
19313 Zero Avenue, Surrey, B.C. V3S 9R9

HANCOCK HOUSE PUBLISHERS
1431 Harrison Avenue, Blaine, WA 98230-5005

(604) 538-1114   Fax (604) 538-2262
(800) 938-1114   Fax (800) 983-2262
Web Site: www.hancockhouse.com   *email:* sales@hancockhouse.com

Contents

CHAPTER FOUR
Areas That I Hiked in Canada Looking for Bears 113

CHAPTER FIVE
Bear Safety Precautions 138

Acknowledgments

I owe my deepest thanks to my mother, Dorothy Scott, who introduced my sister Shirley, my brother Donald (Buster) and myself, to nature at a very early age. The many fishing trips that I went on with my father, Donald (Duke), reinforced my love for hiking and the wilderness.

My family is wonderful, and I am particularly grateful to my wife, Frances, and my sons Donny and Steven, for putting up with many years of my peculiar interests and odd behavior while searching for bears. I would also like to thank Donny and Steven for their help with the preparation of my books.

When I was a young man and working as a fish guardian at Big Salmon River, I learned what it meant to be a conservationist from William Wetmore. His "dedication to nature" is something I have always tried to emulate.

Of all my friends I must thank Jim Kahl for putting up with my eccentric ways. Jim has tolerated my cautious approach in almost everything, except for bears. Jim, I am grateful for all of your help and friendship over the years.

Hanna Patterson is a terrific friend and I appreciate the excitement she brings to hiking in the wilderness. Maria Hall can out hike any woodsman I have met and I just hope I can keep up with her in the future. Joe Kelly is exactly the kind of man you need in the woods. He is funny, friendly and could probably make friends with the biggest bears if he wanted to. Doug Cluff has a strong love for bears and I hope that I emulate his protective approach.

Bill Kirsopp who could be mistaken for my twin brother is fun to be with and I look forward to seeing him every summer. Hoss Palm is a top photographer and I think he speaks bear language. Cas Sowa will do anything to protect a bear and is bound to be successful with all of his nature work. Francis and Mary Trace love fish creek as much as me and any photographer could learn from their patience. Buck and Nancy Maynard are practically royalty at Fish Creek. I would like to thank Robert Small for taking the picture of me that is included within this book. Only I know that Robert has rarely photographed such a fine subject.

I suspect that Virginia Small is one of the keenest bird watchers at Fish Creek but she should remember to occasionally look down in case there is a bear nearby.

Many of the visitors to Fish Creek make my time there more enjoyable. I have been lucky enough to meet some great people that include: Mr and Mrs Jack Foley, Jackie and Bob Gurr, Larry Ward, Pete Gaiser Ron and Kathy Tschakert, Anna Patterson, Matt Donachie, Carl Bradford, Doyle Hickman, Mark Medeiros, Wolfgang Hackman, Pete Ware, Allen Obertreiber, Greg and Joni Wendholt, Richard and Marion Jotcham and Hans Schweizer, Bob and Sue Ann Gay and Ngoc (Kim) Tran.

I have many friends in bear country and if a bear gets me, you will be happy to know that I have not forgotten you. I know you are all waiting for that top equipment I carry and my famous wardrobe you guys are always smiling at. We all know that most of my "valuable" gear should go straight to an antique store or more likely the junkyard. However, I want to remember you all and honor your friendship so I have provided as follows: my cooking utensils are going to Wayne Jones and Terri Scott. Bill (Wild Bill) McCluskey can have my boots. Jackie and Bob Gurr, Virginia and Robert Small can share my hat. Francis and Mary Trace can have my tripod stick and Joe Belanger gets my pack. Jack Foley will receive a pair of my sneakers to remind him of when he played in the N.B.A. Buck and Nancy Maynard will be lucky enough to get my old can of bear spray that I carry around. Bob and Sue Ann Gay will receive my #1 picture, Regina Tuskin will get a close-up picture of me because were about the same age (give or take a few years). Jim Kahl inherits a pair of my socks because he always compliments me by saying I smell like a bear. Bill Kirsopp will get a pair of my pants and a shirt because he likes my wardrobe. As for the rest of you people, you'll all have to fight over whatever is left. Oh yes, Doyle Hickman inherits my bicycle, to be found somewhere between here and Bear Creek Road. Claudia Bloom can have the tree stump she was on when the grizzly charged us. Marlene Metcalf will receive a bird picture. Paul Larkin gets that famous stick that I use to keep the tourists in line. If Mike and Suzi Craft continue to get the bears to behave, then they will get another stick that I have used to swat bears in the rear. David and Vivian Culver will get a can of cooking fluid to remember why they took me to the hospital. Brookside Baptist Church will receive a close-up picture of me to hang down stairs in order to keep the mice and squirrels at bay.

I am also grateful to those members of the public who have an interest in wildlife and in seeing that bears are not disturbed by humans. I would also like to take this opportunity to thank the wildlife of North America, as well as Mother Nature for making this book possible.

Foreword

Having Keith Scott as a father has been quite something. I remember a long time ago watching a spider crawl across a carpet. My father spent 20 minutes trying to get the spider onto a piece of newspaper, and then he carefully took it outside. Then, Dad spent the next 10 minutes watching the spider to make sure it was okay. This is typical of my father's love for nature. Similarly, when hiking in the Rocky Mountains with my father, I recall coming to a lake where careless campers had tossed their garbage into the water. We spent the next few hours wading into the lake and removing the mess. This was one of the many occasions when I realized what it meant to be concerned about nature. I have not met anyone like my father and I admire his dedication to nature.

I grew up believing that all families spent most of their time hiking in bear country, fishing in streams full of salmon, and taking pictures of animals. Some of the best memories, however, are of those moments when I thought I was suffering at the time. I recall being covered in mud after crossing slippery trails, being soaked after sudden downpours, and looking out of my tent to see snow after an unexpected change in the weather. These moments were actually the best because we were usually far from civilization and we would have to cope with the situation as best we could.

One of my earliest memories is of my family wading across a freezing-cold river deep in the heart of the Yukon. Crossing a river with water up to your waist was what I always thought having fun meant -- I was right. Our family has always enjoyed, and endured, the wilderness. My brother Steven has continued the family tradition. When Steven was only nine, he hiked 24 miles (40 kilometers) on one of our typical trips.

My father has taken me to many places that are perfect in their beauty, and I have never seen anything since that is comparable. I am already dreaming of my next trip to Moat Lake, with all of us sitting on logs and warming up to an evening campfire surrounded by snow-covered mountains and a lake that perfectly reflects a starry night.

Although my father leads a curious life, it is both honest and admirable. I can only smile when I think of all the great memories.

—Don Scott

Above - Steven Scott keeping up the family tradition

Left - Donny Scott on another adventure

Introduction

It was another beautiful day in the wilderness. The sort that one takes for granted during a month of hiking through the mountains. It had been windy, but a hiker's greatest enemy, rain, did not show itself. I have shaken my fist at the sky on many occasions in the mountains and have endured many a downpour. I knew, though, that the unexpected is exactly what makes the wilderness so wonderful. On a given day, you might come across a beautiful waterfall, some Indian paintbrush flowers, or spot some bighorn sheep. In that perspective, occasionally hiking with wet feet is not much of a sacrifice.

Although I had a long way to go before reaching my next campsite, I was already picturing a nice fire and a calm night under the stars. The trail had been muddy from prior rainfalls and the sound of my sneakers squeaking slightly as I walked was the only sound. The trail was otherwise good. I have travelled in several areas where the trail can hardly be seen, and instead I have found myself fighting through thick brush. This trail was clear and I was pleased that I only occasionally encountered some mud. There were trees but I was approaching the high country and they were starting to thin out.

Walking on a trail like this gives me time to think and reflect on all the beauty that surrounds me. In the distance, I can see a waterfall and I wonder if that is in the same area as the campsite I am heading towards. I hope so because I might be able to get some good waterfall pictures early in the morning.

Just then, my daydreams vanished, and the nightmare began. I had just taken a slight turn in the trail and a mother bear was standing directly in my path, staring at me, and her cub was nearby. I was awed for a moment, because I usually pick up bear signs or some clue of a bears presence. Today, however, I turned a corner in the trail and there she was. I wondered if it was the wind that may have blown my scent in her direction and made this bear curious.

We were facing each other in a wilderness showdown. I love these animals and I knew that it was my own fault that I had landed in this situation. It certainly was not the fault of the bears because I was deep in their territory. Stumbling across a mother bear with a cub can be dangerous if the mother bear perceives you as a threat. I was dressed as I usually am in the woods. I had on an old pair of muddy sneakers, some ripped hiking pants and an old jacket that was nearly as old as me. My pack was a wooden type that usually provoked laughs from passing hikers. I was an unusual sight in the woods and I sensed the mother bear's curiosity rise as she looked me over carefully.

Even though I have encountered bears on many occasions, the initial instinct is always to run. I know that is an unwise thought because this will only excite the bear, and a grizzly can easily out-run a human. It takes a few seconds for these rationale thoughts to settle in but once they do it has a calming effect. I thought to myself "Keith you are okay and you have been here before. Stay calm don't do anything stupid."

The bear was still looking me over, and as she gazed at my footwear I thought I saw her smile. Her cub was near her but appeared to be nervous at the sight of this strange intruder. The mother took a step forward but the cub did not move. The mother must have known that the cub was not following her, because with-out taking her eyes off me she made the familiar sound "Whoof, Whoof, Whoof." I have heard this sound many times and it is usu-ally in situations such as this where bears are not comfortable with my presence or there is something they are nervous about. The cub reacted to her mother's call, and immediately darted to her mothers side so that they were almost touching each other. The mother bear never took her eyes off me, although the cub was nervously looking around.

I sized the mother bear up, and figured if we got into a tussle I would not do well. She was about as big as any mother bear I had previously encountered and any smile she had over my appearance was gone. She looked tough and unhappy and took another step toward me. I surveyed my surroundings and although there were some trees, there was no obvious escape route. I might be able to make it up a tree before she reached me, but I have seen a grizzly climb a tree and I have not had as much faith in this option as I once had. After pausing for a moment, the bear hunched its shoulders and started coming. This was it.

Could this be the end of my adventures? I tried to tell myself everything was going to be all right, but I was in the unfortunate

Sow Grizzly

position of being able to confirm that every hair on this charging grizzly was standing straight up. I love bears but the sunken face of this grizzly was not handsome. I was hardly in a position to criticize and she probably had similar views about me. Retreat to a tree was now impossible, and the furry terror was only a few steps away, and closing in fast.

I immediately started a ritual that I have developed over several years. It has become one of my essential survival strategies. I try to make the bear think I am a bit nutty which has always been easy to achieve. I looked the bear straight in the eyes and began speaking in my most authoritative voice "Nice bear—I am not going to hurt you." The sound of my voice momentarily startled the bear and for a second she paused and had a quizzical look on her face.

"I am slowly going to back up, and you have nothing to worry about," I continued. The bears face shifted and she squeezed her eyes together.

"I am far from tasty, and I am sure you are not interested in trying me out."

The bear appeared to be through listening to my nonsense. She grunted in a manner that suggested our conversation was coming to an end.

"Take it easy, Take it easy," I pleaded.

The bear was now within a few footsteps and I could feel the effect of her breath.

"Just cool it now, and hold it right there." She was now ready to lunge.

"Stop right there I said," in the loudest voice I could muster.

"That's enough stop it. I am going to leave you. I won't hurt you. Just Take it easy."

I had slowly stepped back while talking and by doing so had created some space between us. The movement was extremely slow and did not startle her any further. This bear was excited and it would not have taken much for her to come all the way. The bear took another step forward and maintained what was an uncomfortable distance from my perspective.

As the bear paused to gather her strength for the coming blows, I offered a quick prayer to Saint Peter, clenched my fist, and closed my eyes and said "That's enough now. You stop right there."

A moment passed. Was I already dead? I peeked. The grizzly and her cub had vanished. Only a few swaying bushes showed that they had ever been nearby. I let out a sound of relief that I have not matched since. This was one of the most dangerous encounters I have had in bear country. I caught my breath and started walking. I continually turned my head but there was nothing in sight. I had survived. Suddenly, the rain began to come down and within a few seconds I was drenched. I was not unhappy though, and I could only smile, as I reviewed the unexpected events.

I have often thought that bears are not well understood, and I find that I am still learning new things about them each time that I go into the woods. I have studied bears in Canada and Alaska since 1967, and I am starting to think that bears understand me. I even occasionally think I can interpret what bears are saying, or what they would like to say. Most of the time, I suspect they are discussing how crazy I am.

Bears of the World

Before I describe some of my wilderness experiences, it will be useful to set out some general information about bears and their habitat.

There are eight species of bears in the world. The spectacled bears are the only bears that live in the southern hemisphere. They got their name from the white fur around their eyes. Because they live in warm temperatures their fur is thin, and since they have a source of food available year-round, they do not hibernate. They are good climbers and have longer legs than other bears. The spectacled bear climbs tall trees to feed mainly on pambili palm.

The Asian black bear is found in Japan and westward to Iran. Its coat is charcoal black with a white v-shaped mark on its neck. When standing, they are about 5 feet (1.5 meters tall). Smaller than other bears, they stay in the Himalaya Mountains during the winter and climb to high elevations during the summer.

Sloth bears live in Sri Lanka and India. They travel at night feeding mainly on insects and fruit. These bears have long fur and very long claws. Often the cubs ride on their mother's back. All other bears have 42 teeth except the sloth bear which has only 40.

The Sun bear lives in Indonesia, Malaysia, Thailand, and Burma. Its name comes from the yellow patch on its chest, and compared with other bears its fur coat is very smooth which gives it a shiny appearance. Sun bears have a long tongue that enables them to eat insects and fruit quite easily.

Panda bears live in China, Tibet and the Himalayas. They have a very human like face and they are almost as cute as me. The Red or lesser Pandas that live in the Himalayas have a reddish brown fur and the ones that live in Tibet and China are larger and have black and white markings. Many people have suggested to me that Pandas are not really bears and that they instead are more related to raccoons. I suspect that the Pandas do not care what we call them.

16

They certainly seem like bears to me and I have a feeling that I would be as cautious of them as I would be of any cute-looking grizzly I might come across in Alaska. They are beautiful creatures.

American black bears can be mostly charcoal black, brown, or white. The white black bears are found in northwestern British Columbia in Canada. They are known as "Kermodes", and native people call them "spirit bears", or "ghost bears".

Black bears live in the forests of central Asia and North America. They stand about 5 feet (1.5 meters). In Canada black bears are found in every province and territory except Prince Edward Island. In the United States, they are found in every state except Kansas, Nebraska, Nevada, North Dakota, Connecticut, Delaware, Illinois, Indiana, Iowa, Maryland, and Rhode Island. There is a healthy population of black bears in the states of Washington, California, and Alaska. In Canada there is a large population of black bears in Ontario, Manitoba, Alberta, the Yukon Territory, and British Columbia.

Grizzly bears are found in Russia, northern Asia, Scandinavia, Spain, Canada, and the United States. At one time, grizzlies lived in many parts of Europe, in Mexico, and in the state of California, but humans have completely exterminated them from Mexico, California, and most of Europe. In the lower forty-eight American states, grizzly bears can be found only in Montana, Wyoming, and Idaho. The state of Alaska still has a healthy population of grizzly bears. In Canada, grizzly bears live in the provinces of Alberta and British Columbia, and both the Yukon and Northwest Territories.

Grizzly bears can be many colors: black, brown, silver-tipped, and a cream colour. Brown bears are grizzly bears although some people find this point confusing, since black bears can be brown! The confusion arises because there can be a striking colour difference and size difference between the bears that live inland and those that live along the coastline. Grizzlies within 50 miles (80 kilometers) of the coastline of North America are usually either light brown, dark brown, or black in colour. Grizzlies found inland can be black, brown and their fur can be silver-tipped to almost white in colour. I have encountered each of these colour variations and a few other unusual exceptions.

On Kodiak Island in Alaska most of the grizzlies are dark brown to black in colour however I encountered one grizzly that was silver tipped.

17

Kodiak bears are also grizzly bears. Some people think that they are a unique type of bear but they are simply grizzly bears that live on Kodiak Island. They are not just any bear however. Kodiak grizzlies are some of the largest grizzly bears in Alaska". They are described in Alaska as "the biggest bears on earth". I have seen some Polar bears of similar size however. The main reason Kodiak bears are so large is that they eat a very rich diet of spawning salmon, and the salmon are available for a longer period on Kodiak Island and other areas nearby than in other parts of the pacific coast line. The salmon in this area have a significantly longer spawning period and this results in a richer diet and some mighty large bears. Kodiak grizzlies have been known to weigh as much as 1500 pounds (675 kilograms).

Grizzly Bear

Polar bears live all over the Arctic region and on the polar ice pack. Some have been known to travel south of the Arctic on ice floes and icebergs. During the winter, their fur is pure white, but in the springtime it turns a creamy yellow. This colour blends in perfectly with the melting ice. Polar bears live in an area of ice and snow for 9 to 10 months of the year, they are flesh-eating animals. Their main sources of food are ringed seals, bearded seals, walrus, guillemots, and other birds. They also feed on berries, lichen, grasses and seaweed when it is available.

Polar bears are at home on the ice, in the water, and along the shoreline. Their bodies are streamlined for swimming and running quickly. The back part of their body is higher, which enables them to run faster. Their neck is longer than other bears. Polar bears have beautiful white fur that is very thick, and this keeps them warm during the freezing arctic winters, and is also an excellent camouflage when hunting and stalking prey. Polar bears listen for the sound of seals under the ice and then they dig them up with their front claws. Polar bears will also wait by a seal's breathing hole for long periods of time (three to four hours). When a seal appears, the bear pulls it through the hole.

Characteristics

All North American bears have certain characteristics in common, some of which contradict popular notions about their habits and their nature. Their eyesight, for example, is often extremely keen. Although bears cannot always make out a stationary object, they can readily detect movement. Another widely-held misconception is that bears are slow and awkward and that they cannot climb trees. In fact, bears are agile.

"I can stand on my head".

Inset - "Hey mother, everything looks different when you look at things this way"

They are also fast and can attain speeds of up to 35 miles (60 kilometers) per-hour. I have seen this speed reached several times when bears have been chasing prey or another bear out of a berry patch. Bears are also good tree climbers. I have also seen an adult grizzly climb a tree and took a photograph to record this very unusual event. Bears react to danger by climbing trees but this is only one of several potential reactions.

North American bears eat just about everything, although some lean more towards a vegetarian diet, while others, such as polar bears, are primarily meat eaters. They all go through a period of winter sleeping but the duration of this hibernation can vary. During this time, the females which are called sows, give birth to their cubs. The cubs are playful and beautiful animals.

"I can juggle".

North American bears are strongly territorial animals, and they generally tend to be solitary rather than social. In the fall of the year, however, polar bears gather together in large groups near Churchill Manitoba and they become quite playful with each other. Bears follow a hierarchy in which a smaller, weaker bear will usually yield to a more powerful one. A notable exception is a sow with cubs. A mother bear will fight even a much larger male, called a boar, with such tenacity that most bears give sows with cubs a wide berth.

Grizzly bear cubs are born tiny and defenseless. They live with their mother for two-and-a-half to three years, although there are some exceptions where cubs stay longer with their mothers. While hiking in Denali National Park, I once encountered a mother and two cubs and both of the cubs appeared to be more than three years old. Black bears normally stay with their mother until they are eighteen months old. The mortality rate among young bears, both grizzlies and black bears, is quite high. Those that reach maturity can expect to live well into their teens and even reach the grand old age of thirty depending, of course, on the behavior of their greatest natural enemy-humans.

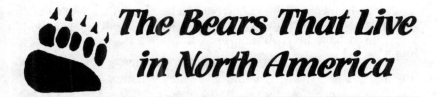

The Bears That Live in North America

Black Bears

The black bear is a massive, bulky animal that can grow to 5 feet (1.5 meters) in length and attain a shoulder height of up to 4 feet (1.2 meters). Because it is such a large animal, many people assume the black bear is also extremely heavy. However, a sow often weighs as little as 150 pounds (68 kilograms) and rarely more than 200 pounds (90 kilograms). A boar is usually a bit heavier than a female black bear. Several exceptionally large black bears have been sighted, including a large boar that was caught and temporarily tranquilized in Riding Mountain Park, Manitoba. Before releasing the bear, the wardens weighed him and were astonished to find he weighed 800 pounds (360 kilograms).

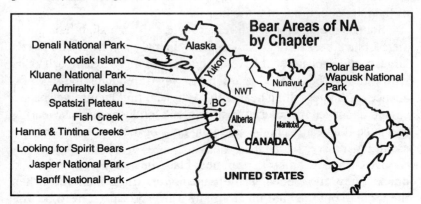

Maps of the main areas that I hiked looking for bears in North America.

Black bears are usually charcoal black, often with a white patch of fur on their chest. They can also be cinnamon, brown, white, and, rarely, black with a bluish tinge. The white bears, whose colour is a result of natural pigmentation—not the deficiency that produces albinos live in British Columbia, while cinnamon colored black bears are most commonly found in the Rocky Mountains and to the west of that region. The black bears that have a bluish tinge colour have been spotted near glaciers in South Eastern Alaska and North Western British Columbia and are called Glacial Blue bears.

Black bears are characterized by a straight profile, a tapered sensitive nose and a long tongue that is very handy when the bear is browsing for food such as ants and small berries. Black bears have an extremely well developed sense of smell that is better than that of human beings. They often stand on their hind legs and sniff the air for any unusual or attractive odors. Black bears have been known to detect the scent of a dead animal from far away, and if the breeze is blowing in the right direction, they can also smell a campfire from a great distance. Hikers would be well advised to keep this in mind when choosing a campsite for the evening.

It has been suggested that black bears have very poor eyesight. This is a myth. My experience indicates that bears can readily detect movement. It is true, however, that they have difficulty making out stationary objects. If a distant observer remains motionless, the bear will usually continue what they are doing and the observer will not be noticed. But a bear that senses motion will approach the source of the movement, out of curiosity.

Sounds are an entirely different matter. Even a slight noise will alert a black bear to the position of an animal or person. The bear's large, round ears are well developed and extremely sensitive. This is why wearing "bear bells" is a popular way of reducing the risk of a chance encounter with a bear and hikers who find themselves near a stream or a river are advised to sing or talk loudly as well as wearing the bells. If a bear hears the annoying bells or the loud talk then they are likely to leave the area.

Despite their bulky appearance, black bears are both agile and quick. They may appear to be clumsily shuffling their feet when they move, but they are far from awkward and can, if need be, run as quickly as 35 miles (60 kilometers) an hour. This makes running from a bear a rather futile and ill-advised exercise. Black bears walk like people with the heel and sole of their feet touching the ground. Black bears have curved claws at the end of their feet, this provides them with better traction and enables them to dig up roots, remove bark from trees, and tear rotting trees apart as they search for insects.

Black bears are excellent climbers, and often clamber up a tree if they are scared or nervous. Inexperienced black bear cubs sometimes attempt to jump off a tree when they are close to the ground. A mother bear who senses danger chases her cubs up a tree, then the sow either joins her cubs up the tree or sits at the bottom of the tree, to protect them. When they climb, the bears grasp the tree with their front paws, then push themselves up by thrusting their hind legs forward. On their way down, they travel backwards, hanging on with their claws. Because black bears do not hesitate to climb trees, hikers should realize that they cannot escape by going that route. Jumping in a lake is also not a good solution. Black bears are excellent swimmers and can make it across large lakes or rivers, provided there is some incentive on the opposite side. They even swim for fun, especially to cool off on a hot day.

Bears love fish, which they catch with great skill, usually sticking to the shallow areas of lakes or streams, where their prey is much more accessible.

Black bears will eat almost anything, but vegetation forms the largest part of their diet. They also eat almost all berries, nuts, insects, fish, small animals, birds, bird's eggs, honey, and grass.

Black bears are exceptionally quiet animals and hikers will only rarely hear them. But there are exceptions, such as two bears I once encountered in southeastern Alaska. These bears were apparently having a dispute over a fishing spot. They had been fishing peacefully a short distance apart, and then they suddenly noticed each other. They approached each other and began to growl and grunt loudly for about four minutes. These sounds normally suggest a certain amount of annoyance on both sides, although in this case no fight broke out.

Bears also use sounds to convey danger. A sow may make a deep "whoof", sound or a whimpering noise if she is concerned for the safety of her cubs, which respond by promptly coming to her side. Black bears that find themselves in trouble make a sound remarkably similar to that of a baby crying.

"Don't bother me when I'm eating grass"

In the fall, black bears react to cooler temperatures and shorter days by searching for a den and preparing for hibernation.

Depending on the terrain, the den of choice could be a hollow tree, a hole dug in the ground on a hillside, or a hole under a tree stump. Some bears even make a crude den by covering themselves up with fallen leaves. Female black bears typically line their den with leaves or other green foliage, while the males, which take to their dens much later, often begin to hibernate only after the first snowfall.

There is a correlation between the number of winter months and the length of time a bear stays in its den. Black bears that live in the far north stay in their dens for five or six months, but those further south emerge much sooner. In Mexico, black bears sleep for only a few days, and some do not hibernate at all. A bear in its den can be awakened by a distracting noise or a period of warm weather. The bear may even wander around outside the den for a while if temperatures are particularly high, but then go back to sleep when the weather turns cold again.

Bears usually live within a very small area of approximately 18 square miles (30 kilometers), within which they develop routes that they use for travelling. Bears are most active early in the evening, during the night, and early in the morning.

With the exception of mating season, black bears are solitary animals and travel alone. At approximately three to four years of age, black bears attain sexual maturity and actively seek out a mate during the months of June and July.

During its first year of life, a newborn cub experiences rapid growth, reaching a weight of approximately 50 pounds (22 kilograms). While cubs are still small enough to be extremely vulnerable, male black bears occasionally try to kill them for food. This is why sows make every attempt to keep boars away from their young. Boars are well aware of the tenacity of sows, and that sows are prepared to fight to the death to protect their cubs. For this reason boars give sows with cubs plenty of room.

A mother black bear looks after her cubs until they are about eighteen months old, at which point she either chases them away or she forces them up a tree and leaves the area. Eventually, the abandoned bears become hungry, begin to search for food and gradually learn to take care of themselves. Black bears can live as long as 25 years, but they do not usually last that long mainly because of their two most dangerous natural enemies — hunters and grizzly bears.

The black bear is a beautiful animal but is best observed and appreciated from a safe distance.

Grizzly Bears

Perhaps one of the most important things to know about grizzlies is that they are endangered in many parts of the world. Humans are responsible for this decline. Hunting and encroaching on the bear's habitat has, for example, eliminated the grizzly population on the Canadian prairies. Because grizzlies have received a great deal of negative press, many people ignore the plight of these animals. My investigations have revealed that most of the negative attitudes about these bears are unwarranted. People do not have the right to destroy animals because they have developed biases against them. I believe that we should promote policies that will reverse the grizzly population decline, so that we can continue to enjoy these magnificent creatures.

Grizzly bears live in a wide variety of areas, both mountainous and coastal, throughout western North America. Inland grizzlies inhabit three mountain zones: the montane zone (valleys), subalpine zone (halfway up mountains), and the alpine zone (mountain tops). Coastal bears are found throughout the Pacific Northwest, and on many coastal islands including Kodiak Island and Admiralty Island in Alaska.

Because of the range of environments in which grizzlies are found, the bears vary greatly in size and colour. There are, however, certain general characteristics. One quick way to distinguish between a black bear and a grizzly is that a grizzly has a pronounced hump on its shoulder. Additionally, a grizzly's front claws are long and prominent, its body hair is long and coarse, and it has a small tail which often goes unnoticed. The hair of a grizzly can be black, dark brown, light brown, grey, or pale yellow. The ends of the hairs are sometimes white or silver, and such a bear is referred to as a silver-tipped grizzly. Grizzly hair can grow as long as 4 inches (10 centimeters). The lush fur coat provides insulation during the winter and helps keep the heat out during the hottest months. Towards late spring, a grizzly sheds its fur and begins growing a new coat. Bears stay cool in the summer by staying in mountainous areas, swimming or resting in the shade.

Below - This Coastal Grizzly is shedding its coat which is light in colour. The new coat that is growing is dark in colour.

Grizzlies located along the northwest coast are often called brown bears, because they are light or dark brown. The term Kodiak bear is used only in reference to a grizzly found on Kodiak Island. Kodiak bears are usually brown, but some can be black or silver-tipped. The grizzlies on Kodiak Island can get to be very large, some weighing in at more than 1500 pounds (675 kilograms), and reaching just over 10 feet (3 meters) in length. The rule of thumb, seems to be that enormous grizzlies are more commonly found in areas within 50 miles (80 kilometers) of the Ocean. Kodiak bears are extraordinarily large because they can catch spawning salmon more than five months of the year.

"This one should do me awhile".

Grizzly holding a stem and eating berries.

Other Pacific coast grizzlies, too, can grow to an impressive size. Coastal bears can feed on salmon for up to four months a year. However, inland grizzlies, which are mainly vegetarian, usually weigh less than 400 pounds (180 kilograms) and grow to about 6.5 feet (2 meters) in length.

As their fishing ability suggests, grizzlies are excellent swimmers and, as I will later explain, at least one adult grizzly I know of is a good tree climber. Grizzly cubs typically excel at both swimming and climbing, but during the second year of a cub's life, the front claws lose their curved shape, inhibiting the grizzly's ability to climb trees.

A grizzly's front claws, five on each foot, can grow to be more than 3 inches (7.5 centimeters) long. This allows the bear to hold berry stems or dig for tubers and burrowing rodents. Excessive digging causes the claws to become short and blunt, but during the inactive months of the winter, the claws continue to grow and sharpness is restored. This pattern is repeated throughout the life of the bear.

This grizzly is sniffing the air and she smells a nearby bear.

A grizzly bear normally has 42 teeth, which can grow as long as 2 inches (5 centimeters). The back teeth have large crushing surfaces that are better for eating plants than meat. Indeed, even though the front teeth are sharp, the overall structure of a grizzlies mouth is more suited to a herbivorous diet. But grizzlies, like all bears, are omnivorous.

The availability of food often determines a bears diet. While their teeth are especially suited for vegetarian fare, they are by no means restricted to vegetables. Instinctively, bears want to vary their diet with meat.

It is just as much of a myth that grizzlies have poor eyesight as it is that any bear has trouble seeing. A grizzly's eyes are small, but they function very well. Grizzlies are able to detect moving objects in the distance and they tend to investigate any unusual activity. On the other hand, if something far away remains still, the bear will have difficulty determining what it is, and will likely ignore it. As well as good eyesight, grizzlies have acute hearing, and any unusual sounds will draw their attention.

Grizzlies use two methods to fish--slow and fast. This grizzly is sneaking up on a salmon.

Grizzlies also have an excellent sense of smell because of their very large mucous membranes. A grizzly's sense of smell is 75 times keener than that of a human being. This ability is extremely useful in detecting either predators or prey. When a grizzly travels, it will often keep its nose close to the ground and continually sniff the air. Even a whiff of something out of the ordinary will prompt a closer look.

A walking grizzly often appears awkward, but this is not the case. If prompted, a running grizzly will use light, bounding gallops and, like the black bear, can move as quickly as 50 miles (80 kilometers per hour). However, a bear running downhill slows up considerably to assure its footing.

The social structure of grizzlies is based on a hierarchy within an independent way of life. Bears are far from communal. Indeed, they are extremely protective of the area in which they live, and will chase away any intruder that wanders into their territory.

A sow grizzly's territorial range covers about 60 miles (97 kilometers). If she has cubs, she drastically curtails her travelling, and as a result, her territorial range. A boar grizzly's territorial range is about 80 miles (130 kilometers), and this area expands during mating season as the male grizzly travels farther afield in search of a potential mate.

The bigger the bear, the more influence it commands. A smaller bear almost always yields to the larger without a fight. Interaction among grizzlies also involves a communication system involving a series of grunting noises, marking territories with their droppings, or leaving scratch marks on trees or on the ground. These warnings reduce the possibility of fights between bears.

This Grizzly is charging up and down the stream to confuse the fish and then he will leap on one.

Sometimes these efforts to ensure privacy coincide with other needs. Grizzlies have to contend with a large population of flies. To deal with these flying pests, they rub up against trees to relieve the itch or until they are covered with sap, which acts as a natural insect repellent. But this practice also offers another benefit, because rubbing against a tree also has the effect of leaving the bear's scent behind and consequently assists in the marking of a bear's territory. If another bear comes near and smells a fellow grizzly, it will sometimes leave the area. If the scent is near food then an intruding bear may ignore the territorial warnings and go after the meal even though this may result in an encounter with another bear. This can arise, for example, near streams that have spawning salmon.

"I will eat almost anything - but not these".

The territories of some grizzlies overlap, which can result in an inadvertent meeting of two bears. If this occurs, the larger bear usually gives chase, sometimes for quite a distance. I have seen these chases go further than a mile (1.6 kilometers). The smaller bear usually retreats to its home territory and will not likely visit the other grizzly again. If there are many grizzlies living in a relatively small area, the bears cut back on the size of their territories in an attempt to avoid encountering each other and tend to be more tolerant of the presence of visiting bears. During the salmon spawning season, bears tolerate each others presence and will often fish only a short distance from each other. Arguments and fights do occur however.

A sow grizzly with cubs will not tolerate a male bear anywhere near her young bears, because of the threat he may pose to her young. Mother bears have a strong love and protective instinct toward their young.

A boar grizzly will kill and eat a cub. All the rules of hierarchy are forgotten when a boar grizzly approaches a mother grizzly. No matter how big he is, the sow grizzly will drive the boar away from the area and even fight him if necessary.

The diet of grizzly bears varies widely, depending on which of the three mountain zones they are inhabiting at any given time. First, it will be useful to set out a brief description of each zone.

The montane zone includes the valley floor and encompasses the meadows and forests. There are many varieties of foliage, including several kinds of berry bushes.

The subalpine zone begins approximately half way up a mountain. This area is characterized by its many meadows and fewer and smaller trees, and by a harsh climate, heavy rain and snowfalls.

The alpine zone is the area close to the mountain tops. Very few, if any, trees grow in this area, but there is a vast array of flowers, including Indian paintbrush, mountain heather, and forget-me-nots. The alpine zone often resembles a spectacular living bouquet.

While certain foods can be found in all three areas, such delicacies as berries are much more plentiful in the montane and subalpine zones. Whereas squirrels, another favorite food for a grizzly, live in the subalpine and alpine zones. Larger animals that might also be prey for a grizzly such as caribou, mountain sheep and goats can be found in all three zones, although the chances of spotting them are better at higher elevations.

In early spring, grizzlies travel along mountain slopes, feeding on clovers, yellow bells, and spring beauties. Their springtime diet also includes grass, frogs, fish, willow catkins, aspen leaves, glacier lily bulbs, cow parsnip stems, and grass roots. The bears will also hunt for newborn deer, caribou, mountain goats, sheep and moose or seek out dead animals that may have been killed during a winter snowslide. Occasionally, a grizzly will strip the bark off of a tree and eat the juicy pulp.

The summer menu is very similar to the spring version, but there are a few scrumptious additions such as shrubs, herbs, wasps, honey, frogs, insects, scats, birds, eggs, burrowing rodents, marmots, dry bear berries, and soopalie berries. Grizzlies appear to enjoy these berries tremendously, despite their sourness, and they are abundant around the middle of July. When the berry crop is poor, bears eat more roots, rich in both protein and minerals. These berries are particularly sought after by bears because they are available most of the year.

The last fall foods for grizzly bears include berries, roots, carrion, grass, squirrels, nuts and fish. For the coastal bears, the spawning salmon are an opportunity of super abundance that allows them to fatten up for the winter. As the berries disappear, grizzlies compensate by increasing their intake of roots and by hunting squirrels more frequently.

Inland grizzlies are usually 85 per cent vegetarian, while coastal bears include plenty of fish in their diet. I have watched

By the fall of the year grizzlies are usually fat and ready for winter.

Grizzlies that live near salmon streams eat as many as eight salmon in an hour. They like just about every kind of salmon: pink, sockeye, coho, silver, and chinook.

Come late September, grizzlies spend less time in the alpine meadows, where the thick snow prevents them from reaching grasses, roots, and squirrels. Squirrels and marmots are also very inactive at this time of year, and this makes it even more difficult for a hungry bear to locate them. Bears will instead look hard for food, often travelling considerable distances to the subalpine and montane zones, where the territory will remain snow-free for a longer period of time. There, grizzlies concentrate on eating fish, grass, roots, and the occasional squirrel.

By the end of October or early November, as temperatures plummet, the entire montane and subalpine zones are covered with snow. Roots and grasses are now inaccessible, and the grizzlies do not have access to their usual food. When the snow falls, they are ready for their winter sleep. Grizzlies then travel to the alpine or subalpine zones and search for a suitable spot to dig a den. An ideal den will be located on a hillside at an angle of about 30 to 40 degrees beneath a canopy of small trees and roots. After finding an appropriate site, grizzlies dig themselves a small cave that will serve as their winter home. Bears are far from claustrophobic; indeed,

Above - Grizzlies mating
Left - "Do you want to box or wrestle?
Neither, I want to give you a hug".

bear dens are usually cramped and are hardly big enough to crawl in and out of. Some bears make their dens cozier by lining them with grass and leaves.

During the hibernation period, the grizzlies heartbeat slows down, and the bears energy requirements decrease. The surplus fat built up during the summer and fall will keep them alive all winter. Bears can sleep for as long as six months without needing to eat. The extra fat also acts as a large blanket, keeping the bear warm as it sleeps.

The winter sleep is long but the bears do not remain motionless. Grizzlies do occasionally move around during the winter; however, the bears do not wake up until warm weather arrives unless they are disturbed. Bears toss and turn when asleep, and the sound of an avalanche or any loud noise near the den will wake a hibernating bear. Residents of Kodiak Island have reported seeing bears roaming around all winter long. Boars and sows without cubs hibernate alone and usually do not leave their dens until springtime. However, they have been seen emerging from their winter dwellings as early as February or March.

During the winter months, grizzlies lose about ten percent or more of their body weight, so finding food is a priority. The abundance of spring foods makes this an easy task, and the bear's lost weight is quickly regained as the yearly cycle begins once again.

"What's that sound mother, Is it another bear?" "Yes stay close to me".

Grizzlies become sexually active between the ages of three and five years. The peak mating season is between May and June. However, I have seen bears mating in July and August as well. During the mating season, boars are able to locate female bears by using their excellent sense of smell. When a boar finds a possible mate, an unusual ritual begins. First, the sow acts nervously in the presence of the boar and runs away only to return and charge the boar. Next, the two bears become playful and begin nuzzling each other. Finally, the bears will become intimate. After the two bears have mated, they lose interest in each another and go their separate ways in search of another mate. Both the male and female bears are promiscuous.

The gestation period for grizzlies is about 255 days. A sow usually gives birth to as many as three cubs every four or five years but occasionally has four cubs at once. Grizzly cubs are born either in January or February, during their mother's hibernation. At birth, grizzlies are toothless, hairless, and unable to open their eyes and they weigh about one pound (.45 kilograms), and rely entirely on their mother to survive, nursing from her and cuddling with her for warmth. A mother will hibernate with her cubs. During hibernation, both mother and cubs survive on the excess body fat that the mother has accumulated before entering her den. Grizzly cubs survive with very little nourishment during the first few months of their lives.

For more than a year, grizzly cubs nurse on their mothers milk, which is extremely rich with about 30 percent fat. While nursing, the cubs follow the mother bear and eat the same foods she does. An eight-month-old grizzly has already started eating grasses, roots, berries, fish, and carrion, imitating its mother and gradually learning to seek out food for itself.

Grizzly cubs usually stay with their mother for two-and-a-half years, and sometimes longer if the sow has not yet found another mate. By the age of two-and-a-half, the cubs have learned what to eat, where to find food, where to dig a den, and how to hunt. The young bears have also found out how to recognize danger and respond appropriately. As the learning period ends, the bear cubs and their mother eat further apart. The grizzly cubs may become permanently separated during this period, or the sow may eventually chase

"Mother, what are you doing"?

the cubs away. In any event, the mother and cubs will finally go their separate ways.

The mother bear will then seek out a boar, and the mating process starts again. The mortality rate for young grizzly bears, like black bears, is extremely high. Approximately four in ten grizzlies have been known to live as long as 25 years or more. A life span in the high teens or low twenties is more common.

I am disappointed with many of the attitudes toward grizzlies that I have encountered. I believe that negative attitudes towards grizzlies are unwarranted and that they are usually supported mainly by those who like to kill for "sport", or those who want to feel superior. If there were no restrictions on killing bears, they would be extinct today. I have no respect for those who brag about having shot bears. There is no honor in shooting a defenseless animal.

It is easy to see why grizzlies have been exterminated from most of their original home range in the world. The greed of humans is the main reason. The media also plays an important role in the extermination of bears, because they sensationalize those rare occasions when a bear attacks a human. The media rarely mention any faults on the part of the humans involved, such as a lack of precautions or the carelessness that is usually involved.

Polar Bears

The polar bear can be found mostly in arctic regions and it differs considerably from the black bear and the grizzly due to its unusually harsh environment. Polar bears have adapted their feeding and hunting habits physically in response to the low temperatures and rugged landscape of their northern habitat.

Polar bears are able to travel extremely long distances, and have been known to follow seal herds for many days. Other journeys begin quite by accident, such as the occasional polar bear that inadvertently hitches a ride on an iceberg and ends up floating as far south as Newfoundland. Polar bears would probably prefer to remain in their new southern home, at least for a while, but they are always rounded up by some meddlesome human, tranquilized and transported back to the north. If it wasn't for humans there would be a healthy population of polar bears south of the Arctic Circle.

Below: "I'm warning you, calm down".

Polar bears vary in size, with some males weighing as much as 1500 pounds (675 kilograms). A more common weight is about 600 pounds (360 kilograms) for boars and considerably less than that for the smaller female bears. They have beautiful fur that can range from pale yellow to pure white, but the nose and much of the face is black. The skulls and necks of polar bears are longer than those of other bears, producing the characteristically prominent frontal area. Their claws are short and sharp and are ideal implements for holding food.

The teeth of polar bears are very sharp and shaped to shear meat, which forms 90 percent of their diet. Their usual prey is the ringed seal; however, they also hunt bearded, harp, and hooded seals. Ringed seals can weigh as much as 150 pounds (68 kilograms)—a gargantuan meal, to say the least. Polar bears hunt seals by first waiting patiently near blowholes in the arctic ice where seals come up to breathe. As a seal emerges, the bear will strike with its sharp claws, then use its powerful jaws to drag the seal out of the water and onto the ice, where the bears meal begins almost immediately.

Polar bears also hunt seals by creeping up on them as they doze on the ice. A bear will first search for a sleeping seal then slowly approach, until its about 100 feet (30 meters) away. Then the skilled hunter rushes forward with long bounding jumps, trying to get between the seal and the only possible escape—the blowhole. The seal will react by heading for the hole but its life will depend upon how quickly it can escape the rushing polar bear. When polar bears are extremely hungry, they will eat the bones as well as the meat, blubber, and skin of a seal. Usually, however, bears will only eat a small portion of a seal. The Arctic Fox provides an efficient clean-up crew.

Male polar bears are dominant in the polar bear hierarchy; however, if a female polar bear with cubs is nearby, no males will approach. As with all bears, the sows are extremely protective of their young and do not hesitate to chase away or fight larger males that may pose a threat.

Polar bears become sexually active between four to five years of age. The mating season begins in April. During this time, male and female polar bears stay in one location for up to several weeks. The sow may have cubs, but this has no effect on her desire to mate.

When a female polar bear becomes pregnant, she leaves the arctic ice and travels to land. They search along the shoreline for a suitable spot to build a den which is usually a cave dug into a snow-drift. The cave will ideally be located along a hillside. In the James Bay and Hudson Bay areas, pregnant polar bears will travel farther inland, often until they reach trees. Those bears will then dig a den in dirt or gravel on the side of a hill.

Polar bears are born in the mother's den during December or January. Litters normally consist of either one or two cubs, although, on rare occasions as many as three are born. At birth, like other bears, the cubs are toothless and hairless, they are unable to see, and they weigh less than two pounds (0.9 kilograms). These delicate creatures depend on their mother to provide sustenance and warmth. The polar bear cubs nurse on her milk until they leave the den in March.

Once out of the den, the education of young polar bears begins, as they imitate the behavior of their mother. When the cubs are a year old, the mother polar bear is still sharing her food with them, but they are learning how to hunt. The cubs stay with their mother for 2.5 years, after which the young bears are left on their own. This is a dangerous time for them, because they are extremely curious and will investigate any nearby noise. Bears that inadvertently approach hunters are making an unfortunate and usually fatal mistake.

As the human population increases in the Arctic, the numbers of polar bears will certainly decline. It is up to all of us to preserve the fragile Arctic environment that supports this playful, strong, and majestic animal.

Pacific Salmon

All bears in North America eat fish. In places where there are no salmon spawning, the bears will catch trout and other fish in shallow areas of streams and lakes. It is very spectacular to see bears catching fish, especially salmon. In some areas that I have been, there are large numbers of Pacific salmon spawning. These areas attract large numbers of bears.

There are six species of pacific salmon. One is exclusively a Japanese species called masu. This salmon exists in the waters from Siberia to the West coast of America and as far South as California.

The sockeye or red salmon normally weighs about 6 pounds (2.7 kilograms), but can weigh as much as 15 pounds (6.4 kilograms). Most of the Sockeye salmon return to the spawning beds where they were born when they reach the age of 4 or 5 years old, although some have been known to stay at sea for as long as 8 years. By the time the sockeye salmon reach the spawning beds, their bodies have tuned bright red while their head and face have turned light green. The male salmon grow a hooked snout and will have long sharp teeth.

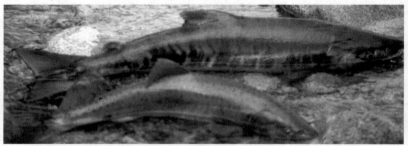

The large salmon is a chum and the small one is a pink salmon.

The chinook salmon which is also known as Tyee, king or spring salmon weighs between 10 and 50 pounds (4.5 -22 kilograms). Some have been known to weigh over 100 pounds (45 kilograms). Chinook salmon stay at sea for up to 8 years.

The coho or silver salmon weighs from 6 to 12 pounds (2.7- 5.4 kilograms). They can, however, get to be 25 pounds (11 kilograms).

The normal weight of a chum (dogfish) salmon is from 7 to 15 pounds (3.1-6.8 kilograms). At Fish Creek Alaska, however, some weigh as much as 30 pounds (13.5 kilograms). When they reach the spawning beds, the chum salmon have vertical stripes of purple and green on the sides of their body. The male starts to form a hooked snout when they are about to spawn and their teeth develop like fangs.

The pink or humpback salmon is the smallest of the pacific salmon. It can weigh from 3 to 5 pounds (1.3-2.25 kilograms). Some could weigh as much as 10 pounds (4.5 kilograms). When they reach the spawning beds their backs are black and their belly turns white. The male forms a large hump on its back and a hooked jaw.

All salmon have some characteristics in common. When the female salmon makes her way back from the sea to the river or stream where she was born, she will find a gravel spot in the stream and start to wiggle her tail to scoop out the fine rocks. This is the process of creating a nest, or REDD for the salmon eggs. She will continue to do this and slowly work up stream. By doing the digging from downstream to upstream, she will cause the current to push the fine gravel into a pile at the lower end of the nest and on the sides. Salmon nests can be 20 inches (50 centimeters) deep. She then releases the eggs into the nest. All salmon species could lay from 3000 - 5000 eggs.

The male salmon immediately goes over the eggs and releases sperm on them. After the male fertilizes the eggs, the female covers the eggs with fine gravel by making a digging action with her tail. The purpose of the eggs being covered with fine gravel is to prevent the current from washing them downstream. This fine gravel also protects the eggs from predators such as birds, other fish and even bears that lick up the eggs on the stream bottom. Both the male and the female salmon will protect the egg bed by positioning themselves overhead. However, within a few days both the male and female salmon become weak and die. One exception is the Atlantic Salmon which does not die at this stage and is able to spawn more than once.

The water current will push dead salmon downstream. Many birds and animals then feed on the carcasses. Bears appear to prefer fresh fish, and I have seen bears ignore dead salmon while trying to catch live ones. If no live salmon are available or if they cannot catch a live fish, which is sometimes the case for younger bears, they will feed on the dead salmon.

The salmon bodies that are not eaten will nourish the plankton and insects that will be consumed by the newly hatched salmon in the springtime. In about 8 weeks the orange-pink eggs hatch. The baby fish stay under the gravel feeding on their yolk sacks for a few weeks before wiggling to the surface. Then, they begin to feed on water fleas and small animals until they are pushed downstream by the high waters in the springtime. The pink and chum salmon go to sea before they are 1 year old. The sockeye go to sea anytime up to the age of 3 years old. The coho go to sea between the ages of 1 and 2. There is evidence that salmon find their way back to where they were born by smell, odor and the taste of the water.

The Main Areas I Hiked in North America

Denali National Park, Alaska

Denali National Park is just West of Highway Number 3 between Fairbanks and Anchorage, Alaska.

Denali National Park

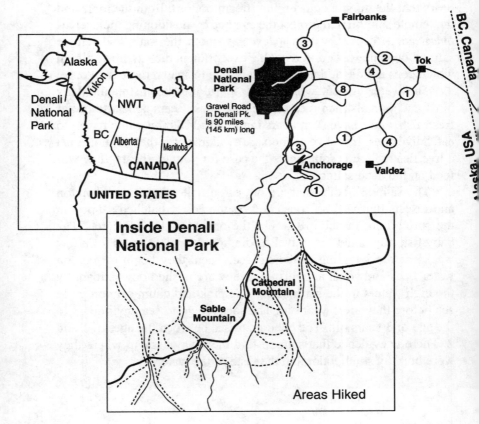

Denali is a very picturesque region of Alaska, and a National Park, which is situated inland between the cities of Anchorage and Fairbanks, is well known for its large bear population.

Park officials at Denali are very safety conscious, and they always urge campers to use the triangle method of camping. With this advice in mind, I began my first hike up Tatler creek. School buses supplied by the federal government take tourists up the 50 mile (80 kilometer) on a gravel road through the park every hour or two during the summer. The round trip takes more than 8 hours.

I got off the bus about one-third of the way along the road, directly north of Cathedral Mountain, and hiked up Tatler Creek. The scenery is spectacular, especially because the area is above the tree line. Most of this park is in the alpine zone, so this is one of the best areas in the world to see grizzlies, caribou, and dall sheep. There are few trees in the area, and I could easily see dall sheep on the high-mountain tops. Blueberries were abundant on the hill-sides, and I knew I was camping where grizzlies would be roaming. I set up camp that evening on a ridge with a marvellous view. I placed my gear well away from my tent and campfire.

The next morning, I woke up to the pattering of a light rain. Dark clouds were blanketing the mountain tops. By noon the sun had beaten the clouds away and I could see the tallest mountain in North America which is Mount McKinley at 20,320 feet (6,194 meters). This mountain is spectacular to look at.

Mount McKinley.

The mountain makes its own weather and a normal summer in Denali consists of rain or snow with the sun appearing every sixth day or so. I hiked down to the stream and followed a trail parallel to a small creek. An adult grizzly emerged from behind a hill and immediately charged me. I stood still, hoping he was just testing me. When the bear was about 70 feet (20 meters) away, he veered off to my right. The charge had been a bluff.

It is not unusual for a bear to come running towards an unwanted visitor, then abruptly stop and retreat. Bears do this to see if the intruder will run, which would be futile, because bears are extremely fast. If I had run, the bear would have become even more excited and would soon have had me for lunch. It is difficult to remain calm as you watch a charging bear, but this is the key to survival.

The grizzly was now beside the stream, and behind him I noticed a caribou carcass. This explained why he had charged. My presence was perceived as an intrusion into his feeding spot, and he was trying to scare me off. I had interfered with him as he dined, and I, like any other animal that might have inadvertently wandered into his territory, had to be dealt with.

I slowly backed away to a nearby ridge, where I could safely observe the bear and his meal. I noticed blood on the caribou. This meant that the bear had probably killed the animal within the past few hours. A few moments later, a silver fox strolled along the shoreline of the creek. The bear saw it and charged. I sympathized with the fox. Nevertheless, the fox quickly retreated and the bear returned to his food.

Fifteen minutes later, the fox was back once again. Apparently it had not understood the first message-or else it was too hungry to care. The grizzly, unaware that the interloper had returned, continued to eat. The fox moved around the grizzly and began to approach from the opposite side. This foolish fox was trying to sneak up on the carcass, but all that he managed to do was get himself into a face-to-face encounter with the grizzly. This time, all the bear had to do was glare at the pesky would-be thief, which finally clued in and retreated, making its way upstream through the bushes. Tired of being disturbed, the grizzly laid down and went to sleep. The sun was dipping below the mountains, so I returned to my campsite.

The next day, the familiar looking clouds were back. I kept an eye on the threatening sky as I began to hike along the bank of the Toklat River. I was now 11 miles (18 kilometers) from Tatler creek with spectacular alpine meadows in any direction I chose to hike. I was on a steep, grassy slope when I noticed a grizzly standing on his hind legs about 100 feet (30 meters) away. He looked at me for a moment, then dropped down and headed out of sight. This encounter was not as exciting as the day before, but better than nothing.

I continued hiking and was in front of a grassy knoll, when I heard a grunting noise. Two young grizzlies appeared and began walking towards me. I slowly began to move to my left, but even this controlled movement excited one of the bears, which broke into a run. When he was 40 feet (12 meters) away, I realized he was not bluffing. This bear was going to come all the way.

I immediately dropped to the ground and protected my head with my hands and arms. This was more excitement than I had counted on. The bear was right beside me, and I was an easy target. I didn't smell very appetizing perhaps, because after the bear had sniffed most of my body, he ran to the hill-side to join his companion. I was very nervous, but I sat up. The 2 bears were still within sight, but in a few moments they had both disappeared. It took me several days to stop shaking.

Later that week, while I was hiking near the Sable Mountains, I spotted a grizzly sow with 2 cubs. Fully recovered from my previous encounter, I watched the family with keen interest. They were feeding on some nearby grass and berries, but the sow appeared agitated and began pacing rapidly, her nose close to the ground. Then she got extremely excited, stood on her hind legs and looked intently at some rocks. The quick movements of the mother bear got the cubs excited too, and they began to circle their mother.

"Stay here and I will try to catch that squirrel".

45

Finally I figured out what the mother bear was looking at. Among the rocks was a ground squirrel, frantically darting away from the bear, as she jumped around the area in an attempt to trap her quarry. But the speedy squirrel had already made its getaway. The dissatisfied bear continued to sniff the rocks, attempting to regain the scent, but it was no use. At last, all 3 bears calmed down and went back to the berry-and-grass picnic.

I was not the only one watching these bears. On the hill-side, not far away, an adult grizzly boar was nervously keeping an eye on the events below. The boar was shedding his fur, and he looked rather shaggy, but the coat would grow back before cold weather set in. Finally, the boar began to move away, glancing back periodically to make sure nothing was coming after him.

A few days later, I was hiking early along the shore of the Toklat River when I came upon another sow grizzly with 2 cubs, and they were all feeding on soopalie berries. The 2 cubs were extremely large and were almost as big as their mother. She was close to 300 pounds (135 kilograms). These cubs would be on their own soon. The way the 3 bears were eating was a clue. The cubs occasionally approached the berry patch where the sow was feeding, but she clearly disliked this idea and stared at them forbiddingly whenever they approached. Faced by that cold stare, the offending cubs backed up and went to look for another berry patch. When it was time to leave, the sow took the lead and the cubs followed, about 30 feet (9 meters) behind her. This gap was yet another indication that the sow wanted more space and that the cubs would soon be on their own.

Not long afterwards, a grizzly boar came over to sample the soopalie berries. Something was bothering this bear. He walked over to a flimsy tree, turned around, and scratched his rear end against the trunk. Then he turned his attention to his upper back, giving it a good long massage against the rough bark. I could see from his big smile that this grizzly was really enjoying himself.

While this was going on, a large sow with 2 yearling cubs walked into an adjacent berry patch. This was trouble brewing. The presence of the other bear was clearly making the cubs nervous. Every few moments, they stood on their hind legs and looked around the area while the boar, his scratching done, went back to the berries, unaware that he was getting closer and closer to the bear family.

When he was within 40 feet (12 meters) of the cubs, the mother bear became furious and charged.

The chase was on and both bears went galloping like racehorses towards a nearby hill. This is the fastest that I have ever seen a grizzly move. I would estimate that they were both running about 35 miles (56 kilometers) an hour. Not until the boar had run up the hillside did the sow stop her pursuit and return to her cubs.

With their mother back safely, the cubs became playful, batting each other with their front paws, then they stood on their hind legs and started wrestling. The bear family walked to another berry patch and the antics continued as the cubs tried to splash each other in the river. The mother bear, uninterested in the game, sat in the water and tried to cool off.

The grizzly sow was aware of my presence. At one point she stood on her hind legs and stared in my direction and was clearly unhappy that I was watching her. Then she began to walk my way. After seeing what had happened earlier, I knew this bear was protective. It was definitely time for me to leave. I slowly backed away, looking back after about 5 minutes. No bears were in sight.

I had hiked a long distance when I saw a caribou bull resting on the trail. He was enormous, with a large set of antlers. I had to wonder how he could see with those great prongs growing right in front of his eyes. I suppose he had to get used to seeing the same view. I continued on, happy to have had such an excellent day viewing animals.

The next morning, I woke up early and was surprised that there were no clouds. But I suspected they were somewhere waiting for me. I was about to begin hiking when I noticed a grizzly feeding on blueberries, so I watched him eat. An hour later, he finally had his fill, and sat down for a rest. It is always comical to see one of these massive creatures in a sitting position. But what made this one particularly amusing was that he was scratching himself at the same time. Insects often burrow into a bears fur, causing a powerful itch, which the bear relieves this by using its claws as a digging tool to remove the bugs.

As the grizzly was departing, he came face-to-face with a younger bear, which he immediately charged. The young bear turned and ran up the hill-side, his pursuer right behind him. The chase lasted for about 10 minutes. Finally the boar had to give in to the swiftness of youth. He may have been big, but he was not very fast.

Moments later, I heard a "WHOOF". I turned around and discovered I was not alone. Next to me in the berry patch was a large grizzly, who-for the time being--was staring at me. The warning sound was an indication that this bear did not want me in the area. I complied with his wishes and slowly moved away. Just as I escaped, a familiar storm cloud moved overhead and dumped its load on me. I think nature was trying to tell me something, but I'm not sure what it was.

The nights were becoming cooler now, and this made the wet, cloudy days even less tolerable than usual. However, the damp weather could not extinguish the beauty of the foliage. The once green grass had mellowed to become a bright gold, and the willow leaves were turning orange and were tinged with red. The landscape was like a rainbow, and the pot of gold was just being there to witness it.

It is during this time of year that members of the deer family rub the velvet skin off their antlers. For the bears, this is feasting season. With winter approaching, it is time for bears to load up on food. The blueberry crop is starting to diminish, and the bears turn to soopalie berries, legumes, and bear roots as a staple of their daily diet. In addition, they begin to spend more time chasing ground squirrels to supplement the roots and berries.

A few days passed before I saw another bear-a grizzly sow with 2 yearling cubs. They were walking across a meadow early one afternoon, stopping every once in awhile if they spotted some blueberries. The cubs seemed more interested in playing than eating. Whenever they were within striking distance of each other, a chase would commence and the young bears would wrestle each other and roll around on the ground. As a finale, they would bat each other with their paws. Then it would start all over again.

The sow, unconcerned with the cubs shenanigans, sat down next to a berry patch and began eating. She periodically lifted her head and looked in the direction of the cubs, but after assuring herself that they were alright, she would turn back to her feast. Eventually, the mother bear stood up and began walking across a slope; then, with a sudden burst of speed, she broke into a run, stopped abruptly, and hit the ground with her front paws.

The object of all this attention was a series of squirrel holes, about 2 meters away. Slowly, the sow approached the burrows, her nose close to the ground, then once again she darted forward and skidded to a stop. Her best efforts proved inadequate that day, and it seemed that these bears would have to be content with a supper of berries.

Meanwhile, the cubs were trying to catch up to their mother. When they reached her side, all 3 started walking downhill, towards Sanctuary River. The water was quite high, but the 8 month-old cubs and the sow had no trouble crossing. On the other side, there was a large patch of soopalie berries, and soon the bears were enjoying a big meal.

After sampling the berries, the sow wandered over to a nearby tree and tried to relieve her itchy back. The cubs watched, then followed her and started rubbing against adjacent trees as their mother sat down and began to roll in the fine gravel beside the water. All of a sudden, the sow uttered 2 low pitched grunting sounds, and the cubs quickly ran to her side.

Next, the 3 bears began to walk toward me, and they were all looking in my direction. The cubs appeared nervous, and one of them stood on its hind legs behind the sow. When she was about 20 feet (6 meters) away, I slowly backed up, hoping that I would not excite her. The sow walked over to where I had been standing, and then began to feed on berries. Her actions conveyed a message to me, and I received it loud and clear. If I had not responded as she wished, I am certain that she would have moved me herself.

One of the most interesting aspects of this bear family was the method of communication between the sow and her cubs. Each time the sow made 2 low grunts, the cubs immediately came to her side. During the period I watched them, the cubs never ignored this command, and to tell the truth, I wouldn't have either.

The sun was beginning to set. I was still facing a 2 hour hike back to the tent, so I decided it was time to go. I took one last look at the 3 bears, then set out on my journey. Along the way, I had to cross Sanctuary River. The water had risen considerably, and I knew what to expect. I could do nothing but clench my teeth and wade in. It was terribly cold, and the water was over my knees, and worst of all, I almost got swept away by the strong current. It took all my strength and balance to stay on my feet. Crossing streams and rivers has never been one of my favorite activities, and this experience reinforced my attitude.

The next day, I spotted the same grizzly family in an alpine meadow. My presence made the bears nervous, and soon they were all running away. The grizzly sow was quick, and the young cubs were unable to keep up, although they ran as fast as they could. Eventually, the sow slowed down and took a look behind her. Because I was farther away, she came to a halt and waited for the cubs.

When the cubs got to her side, she laid down and rolled over on her back. The cubs crawled on top of her and began to nurse. From my vantage point, the bears looked like a large boulder. The nursing lasted for about 3 minutes, and then the sow got up on all fours and led her family away. I watched until all 3 bears disappeared over a hill.

The next morning, a light rain was falling in the valley, and as I hiked into the meadow, it started to snow. After about 4 hours, the sun finally broke through, the clouds dissipated, and I got a clear view of Mount McKinley.

Animals walking in winter landscapes are wonderful to watch. In a valley below, I noticed 2 caribou bulls pushing away snow with their hoofs, attempting to clear a small patch of grass to feed on. Their antlers were magnificent.

Two bull Caribou

A few hours later, a chocolate-colored grizzly walked in front of me, and, like the caribou, cleared a patch of grass with his front paw and began to eat. This bear did not object to my presence; in fact, he ignored me as he filled up on grass then ambled away.

I stayed in the area for another night, but when I awoke, a snowstorm was in full swing. Nature's message was loud and clear, so I packed up my gear and returned to civilization. It had been an excellent trip, despite the weather.

Kodiak Island

I got on the ferry in the town of Homer, Alaska and arrived in the city of Kodiak late at night. The city of Kodiak is located on an island with the same name in Alaska. The weather was overcast the day I arrived, and I soon found out that the weather in this area is typically cool and wet. About two-thirds of Kodiak Island is a wildlife sanctuary called the Kodiak National Wildlife Refuge which was established in 1941 primarily to protect the large population of Kodiak bears.

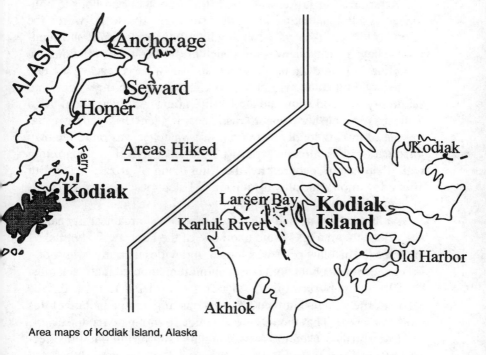

Area maps of Kodiak Island, Alaska

Boar grizzlies on Kodiak Island are enormous and have been known to weigh as much as 1500 pounds (685 kilograms). Their bodies are also long and can extend to over 10 feet (3 meters) in length. I knew that if I had any close encounters in this area I would have to climb an extremely large tree. Before I could plan any routes of escape from bears unhappy with my presence, I had to find some.

51

The best areas to photograph bears were only accessible by float plane, and my meagre budget forced me to find an alternative route. I ended up hitching a ride on a mail plane that was travelling to the isolated village of Larsen Bay which is an excellent area to see bears.

While we were airborne, I surveyed the rugged landscape and concluded that the terrain would be almost impossible to negotiate. The forest was just too dense for hiking. As a result, I decided to hike on established bear trails and along the shores of the salmon streams. This approach would also dramatically increase my odds of seeing plenty of bears. This is always my primary aim.

After arriving in Larsen Bay, it took me about an hour to convince myself that hiking along the shoreline would be worth the effort. It looked like pretty rough going with dense brush surrounding the bay, but the tide was out which meant I could travel along the shoreline so I gave it a try. It wasn't so bad. When I reached the end of the bay, I hiked about a mile (1.6 kilometers) into the woods, and set up my tent and soon had a campfire going. As I was about to go to sleep, some bushes began to rustle near my tent. I started my usual routine of talking loudly to scare away whatever was out there. My imagination was running wild, as I pictured myself   quarreling with, then being devoured by, the King Kong of grizzly bears. But after a few moments, all was quiet, and I slept peacefully for the rest of the night.

At dawn, I got up and had a look around the area near my campsite. Close to the tent, I came upon one of the largest grizzly tracks I have seen. The claw print was longer and wider than my own foot. , I imagined an elephant with claws until I remembered that track must have been left by last night's visitor. I considered running for the safety of the village, but then I had visions of getting a picture of this monstrous bear. That thought was enough to motivate me to stay.

I nervously picked my way along the trail, heading in the direction of the Karluk River. Along the way, I saw a small brook-fed pond where small fish were jumping. There seemed to be 100 fish in the air at any given moment. I was uncertain if they were trout or salmon, but it was quite something to behold. A few miles further on, I came upon a less welcome sight. There was a big patch of bog, which I reluctantly waded through as there was no turning back. Every true lover of the wilderness knows the feeling of getting his feet wet on the trail.

I arrived at the Karluk River and I could see that there were quite a few chum salmon and silver salmon splashing as they swam upstream. There were several dead salmon along the riverbank, and I knew this would attract bears, so I began to move very slowly and cautiously. These fish had been caught by bears, partially eaten, and were then discarded. The tastiest portions of the salmon including the skin, brain, and eggs had been consumed. There were no grizzlies in sight, but I had a feeling they were nearby. With all this food swimming around, they would certainly be back.

Several bald eagles were flying overhead, dipping down to dine on the leftover fish. I watched the majestic birds and waited around for a few hours, but the only other animals I saw were 3 deer that had wandered out of the forest to have a drink in the river. They waded out in the water for only a moment, and then nervously looked in the direction they had come from and suddenly they jumped out of the water and took off through the bushes. I tried to figure out what was worrying them, and although nothing else emerged from the dense underbrush, I had an odd feeling that something was lurking back there, just out of sight.

I decided to continue hiking and tried to be as quiet as possible. However, I was unable to keep the branches and twigs from rustling and snapping as I moved. I thought to myself that I might be better off walking on the bear trail that ran beside the river. It's rare to think that walking on a bear trail is a good option to take when something unknown may be nearby. In any event, I returned to the area where I had watched the deer run into the bushes. As I scanned the brush, I suddenly noticed the rear end of a grizzly.

It's rear end was so big that I blinked to reassure myself that I wasn't hallucinating. If this was the back, I was scared to see the front. In fact, of all the rumps I have ever observed, and I have seen some big ones, this was the largest. Imagine a furry Toyota, and you will have a good idea of this bears backside. I considered taking a picture, but perhaps it was unwise to expose impressionable school children to such a spectacle. Before I could make up my mind, the bear started moving away and, despite its size, I could not see where it was going. Just then, the bushes began to rattle to my right. Could this bear be circling me?

Fearing the worst, I went down to the river and waded into the cold water. I started heading upstream while frequently glancing back every few moments to see if I was being followed. I could detect no signs of the bear anywhere. After wading in the water for about 10 minutes, I felt safe, so I rejoined the bear trail and headed back towards Larsen Bay.

On the way back, I noticed several deer dart away from a meadow where they had been grazing. Just ahead of me, there were 2 brown and white foxes that had apparently caused a disturbance. Seeing these less dangerous animals restored my courage, and I became more determined than ever to get some good bear photos. I decided to continue hiking toward Larsen Bay, but I would search carefully for a promising spot to see bears along the way. I was feeling bold once more so decided to camp in the area again. As I neared the community, I came to a stream full of pink salmon. This would be a prime bear watching spot. Grizzly tracks were everywhere, and there were 2 bear trails leading out of a nearby thicket that led down to the stream. One of the paths had been used so frequently that it was padded down like a dirt road.

Early the next morning, I was safely positioned up a lookout tree near the stream when a light-brown grizzly sow, weighing about 200 pounds (90 kilograms), wandered out of the bush and walked over to the stream. She lost no time getting her breakfast. After a single lunge into the water, she emerged with a small bright salmon in her mouth. Obviously famished, she returned to shore and ferociously tore the fish to pieces, ignoring the pesky magpies flying overhead and which occasionally landed nearby, waiting for leftovers. The fish was soon devoured and the grizzly returned to the stream, where she sat down to cool herself off in the icy water. She rolled in the shallow stream and thrashed around, and then stood up and shook herself dry. Eventually, she caught another fish and carried it into the woods. This was a good start, and I was glad to get some pictures from the safety of my lookout tree.

A few uneventful days passed, and finally my patience was rewarded. On the third evening, two chocolate-brown grizzlies emerged from one of the trails, each weighing about 600 pounds (270 kilograms). It was too dark to get any decent photographs, but I was thrilled to see those enormous bears.

It was another couple of days before the sound of snapping twigs in the woods signalled the presence of another bear. This one was a silver-tipped grizzly wandering along one of the bear trails.

I was surprised by its colour, because most grizzlies on the island, or at least those living near the coastline, are dark or light brown. But there are always some exceptions, as this magnificent bear proved.

The following week, the weather turned cold. The grass and leaves were tinged with yellow, and a frosty wind blew in with a vengeance. One morning, as I approached my leafy lookout, I was startled by the sound of scratching. To my amazement, I saw a adult grizzly climbing up a cottonwood tree about 200 feet (sixty meters) away. This bear climbed more than 20 feet (6 meters) before reaching the first limb, where it stopped to rest. I was also surprised to see how easily the bear climbed. This bear was shifting its enormous bulk with considerable grace and hugging the tree with its paws as it moved upwards. Wildlife officials have repeatedly told me that adult grizzlies cannot climb trees, because their front claws are too long and not curved enough. This bear obviously did not realize it couldn't climb a tree.

I got so excited about recording this extraordinary sight on film that I ran toward the tree. I was just in time to see another grizzly boar come out of the bushes near the tree, heading in my direction. I stopped, stood my ground, and hoped the bear would not become disturbed about my presence and charge me. That would be like being attacked by a tank. This grizzly weighed over 1100 pounds (455 kilograms), which was more than 3 times as much as the bear who had gone up the tree. When the boar on the ground got within 35 feet (10.5 meters) of me, he stopped, turned and faced the opposite direction, and then slowly lumbered over to the other side of the tree where the other bear was watching us both from high above.

I realized that the large boar had been chasing the smaller bear, which might have inadvertently wandered into his pursuer's territory. But I don't think the bigger grizzly was expecting the intruder to come up with quite the escape route that it chose. I'm not sure which of us was more amazed--me or the enormous bear at the base of the cottonwood.

I tried to move into a better position for taking photographs, but my movements prompted the boar to shift his attention from the treed grizzly to me. I didn't think my heart could survive another approach from this huge creature, so I kept still, and he went back to watching the other bear. We all waited for about 10 minutes for something to happen. Meanwhile, I was vigorously snapping pictures. Finally, the large boar stood up and gave me a grimace before wandering away. After a moment, he had disappeared into the dense vegetation.

With the big boar out of the way, the treed grizzly focused his attention on me. He gave me a look of disgust. I reacted to the disapproving look by slowly backing away from the tree, and the grizzly began climbing down. The bear descended rump first, with its paws hugging the tree. This was not a particularly elegant sight, but effective climbing just the same. When the bear reached the bottom, it stood on its hind legs, put its front paws against the tree, and then took a good look at me. The grizzly seemed to be grinning, although this may have been my imagination. After a moment, the bear dropped down on all fours and quickly wandered away.

This unusual experience made it difficult for me to sleep for several nights, but I stayed in the area in the hopes of seeing those bears again. Early one afternoon, I spotted the large boar sleeping on the side of a bear trail, not far from where we had met previously. I watched him for awhile, keeping well back. Occasionally, he lifted his head and sniffed the air, then went back to sleep. After about 40 minutes, the bear rose and casually walked away. This was a much tamer encounter than our earlier meeting.

The weather was getting extremely bad, so I headed back to Larsen Bay. When I got to the village grocery store, a lady asked me if I was "the bear man". I was uncertain why she was using that term, but I replied that, yes, I did enjoy photographing and studying bears. Apparently, news of my hobby was widespread, and several other residents approached me to inquire about the bear sightings I had made. I heard the term "bear man" from the villagers quite frequently, and I thought it was funny, and it was only later, as I was about to board the plane home, that I discovered that the joke was on me. To my great embarrassment, I realized the entire rear end of my pants had been torn away. I had been wandering around town with my underwear in plain view. I wondered if they really meant "bare man", rather than "bear man", although I guess both terms fit.

As I left the area, I recall thinking how glad I was that I had come. Despite the rugged terrain, I had managed to get some incredible photographs, including the rare image of an adult grizzly up a tree. I had also witnessed what must have been the world's largest bear buttocks.

Admiralty Island

Juneau, is the capital of Alaska, and the only way to get there is by ferry or plane. After hiking around Juneau for a few days, I caught the ferry for the village of Angoon on Admiralty Island. This island is very wild and is quite large although it is smaller than Kodiak Island.

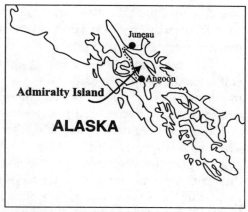

Admiralty Island Alaska

It has a reputation for having an extremely large grizzly population. I used to wonder how bears reach Islands such as this and I have suspected that they may have crossed on ice a long time ago.

The small ferry landed at Hood Bay which is on the West side of Admiralty Island. When I made it to the head of Hood Bay I quickly realized I was here at the right time, because in early September the streams flowing into the bay are full of spawning salmon.

Grizzly tracks, diggings and partly eaten fish were everywhere along the creeks. These signs were a good indication of a healthy bear population. The reputation of the Island was well deserved it seemed to me even though I had not yet spotted a bear.

After four days of watching and hiking, I headed in a northerly direction to the top of a mountain. I had an animal trail and the terrain was pretty clear. The closer I got to the mountain the more I could see. When I reached the top of the mountain, the scenery was beautiful as I could see Hood Bay and in the distance the Pacific Ocean. There were no bear tracks, scat or diggings in these high meadows. One reason for this is that on Admiralty Island there are no ground squirrels, marmots, pikas, caribou or black bears. With very little food for bears up here at this time of year the bears will instead head for the spawning beds which are full of food.

I started the return journey to Hood Bay, and after a few hours I spotted a sow grizzly and cub making their way towards a salmon stream. The sow and 8 month old cub were fat and in good shape.

The colour of their fur was dark brown to black. The sow stared at me momentarily, then both bears moved slowly in the opposite direction and were soon out of sight.

The next morning, I was hiking along the mouth of Hood Bay and I heard coughing sounds out in the water where the bay meets the Pacific Ocean. I could see that humpback whales were feeding nearby. I was so excited that I began running along the shore in the direction of where they were going. There were at least 13 of them. They would dive down under a school of fish, make bubbles in a circular pattern that resembled a net to confine the fish into one area, then with their mouths open the whales made their way to the surface taking in as many fish as they possibly could. When the whales surfaced in a group some of their bodies were half way out of the water while others had their heads just above the surface. It was the most fascinating thing I had ever seen.

Humpback whales can grow to be 53 feet (16 meters) in length and weigh as much as 40 tons (18,000 kilograms). They are black and have a white throat and chest. A humpback whale head is large and his neck and eyes are small. The nostrils or blowholes are located on the back of it's body. They have flippers and a tail called a fluke, which is their major means of movement. Whales only have a few body hairs.

Humpback whales are members of the baleen family of whales. They have no teeth. The name baleen is derived from the formations that grow from the roof of their mouth and hang down in large

Whales singing

sheets forming plates. The outer edges of the baleen are smooth while the inner edges are like fibers and serve as strainers. When a whale is feeding it takes in water and food. The water is squeezed out the whales tongue while the food is caught on the inner surface of the baleen.

A humpback whale food consists of crustacean, plankton and small fish. During the winter whales live in warm water while in the springtime they migrate to northern waters where they stay for the summer months.

The whales made their way along the coastline in a southerly direction and were soon out of sight. I really enjoyed my trip to Admiralty Island even though I only saw a few bears. The whales made up for this.

Fish Creek, Alaska

Fish Creek bear sanctuary is located across the border from Stewart, British Columbia, and 4 miles (6.2 kilometers) north of the village of Hyder, Alaska. Stewart BC is readily accessible by car from Highway 17 (Yellowhead Highway), that goes from Prince George to Prince Rupert. 43 km West of New Hazelton, turn North along the Cassiar Highway (Highway 37) for 170 km. Once at Meziadin Junction, head west on Highway 37A, past the spectacular Bears Glacier and on to Stewart BC, and Hyder

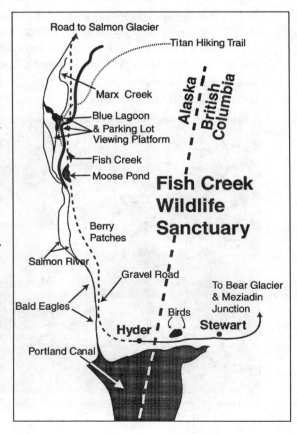

AK. The permanent population of Hyder is less than 100. Many visitors describe Hyder as a ghost town but it would be more accurate to describe it as a many-grizzly town. This is one spot where almost every visitor is likely to see a bear if they want to.

The village of Hyder is located near the mouth of the Salmon River and is surrounded by several large green mountains, with a few that are snow-capped. One word can explain both the beauty of this area, the people and the bears that live there-- Magnificent.

The sanctuary is renowned for the many salmon that spawn in Fish Creek and Marx Creek. These salmon attract hungry black bears and grizzlies. Because the bears are protected, they thrive here. In fact, the bear population is so large that the residents of Hyder are used to seeing both grizzlies and black bears roaming through their town. Normally, the mixture of bears and people is bad for bears, but Hyder is a special place, where they usually coexist quite peacefully. Those that take precautions should be okay.

The magnificent Salmon Glacier is also nearby and is accessible to vehicles. The drive takes approximately one hour from Fish Creek and it is one of the largest, and most spectacular glaciers in the world, well worth seeing.

Stranded Iceberg at the toe of Salmon Glacier. "Can you see me?"

Salmon Glacier

At the "toe" of the glacier is Tide Lake, which is really a part-time lake formed in the winter as ice accumulates and creates a dam that prevents any water from escaping. The water's silty white colour makes it an unusual sight. As the weather becomes warmer, the dam eventually breaks and the water flows towards Fish creek and Salmon River.

Once the water has left Tide Lake, the icebergs that were once floating now sit on dry land, and one can easily walk among them. Some of these stranded icebergs are enormous, and when walking near them during warm days, you need to constantly look up in case any big chunks are about to break off. Searching for bears has led me to some very strange places, and the valley of stranded icebergs is one of them. The landscape is eerie.

The protection officers at Fish Creek are among the best I have met anywhere. They love bears as much as I do, but there is always a chance that a bear may get aggressive. The officers carry and use bear spray whenever necessary. Shotguns are available but so far they have never had to use them.

The officers and regular visitors that come to Fish Creek every year have become so familiar with the bears living here that they have given them nicknames. Some of the bears are Harold, Mahogany, Shadow, Sugar Sow, Brown Pants, Big Ears, Scotty, Fluffy, Big Buck, Nancy, Laura Lee, Alex, Harriot, Ossy, Hugo, Bill and Festus.

Festus was the local favorite because he walks with a limp, although he has not been spotted for several years.

Fish Creek is the promised Land for anyone that appreciates nature. Gulls and bald eagles continually fly over the creeks, and below them the salmon splash and struggle against the current. This habitat is filled with sound, and the noise creates a wonderful symphony. It is amazing to watch fish during the spawning period, and each time I see this process, I appreciate life a little more.

Three species of salmon spawn in Fish Creek: chum salmon, pink salmon and coho. It is immediately apparent to a visitor why bears along the coastline are so large and magnificent. This rich salmon diet causes the bears to gain weight quickly.

I hiked along the shore of Fish Creek occasionally glancing at the water to watch the salmon swimming upstream. On the shoreline were several decaying fish carcasses-a repulsive smell, as far as humans are concerned, but judging from the reaction of birds and bears, it must have some delightful qualities. For me, the sight of rotting fish is a signal to take a wide detour. The noise along that shoreline was continuous; slapping, splattering, and splashing of the salmon drowned out any sounds that nearby birds or animals might be making.

I knew there were bears in the area, so I tried to be much more aware of any activity out of the ordinary. Of course, when you are this far from civilization, everything seems out of the ordinary.

I continued walking until I approached an area with shallow spawning beds, where I could easily see the backs of chum salmon sticking out of the water only about 3 inches (7.5 centimeters) deep. On the other side of the stream, I noticed 2 bear tunnels among some bushes; these distinctive passages are well-used trails that go through very thick brush and are often covered with brush at the 4 foot (1.2 metre) level. If I were patient, there was a good chance that a bear would eventually come out of one of these tunnels.

Scouting around for a good lookout spot, I came upon a bear trail on the shore that led from the creek to the tunnels, both sides of which were littered with fish remains, likely discarded by bears. To compensate for splashing noises coming from the creek, I would move for a few moments, then pause to listen for any large animals that might be nearby. I had to be especially careful when I approached turns, not knowing what could be lurking around each bend.

I was still within sight of the bear tunnels, and had just been listening intently for a very long moment, when I was suddenly confronted by a bear. My ears are evidently not what they used to be, although my ways of thinking remain the same. Perhaps this was my problem. In any case, the black bear was only about 25 feet (7.6 meters) away. He began to walk towards me, so I responded by talking to him: "I'm right in front of you." He hesitated, then kept on coming. I was running out of options, so I pointed my tripod at him and, in a gruff voice, said, "Don't come any

"I got you".

closer." The bear stopped again. Maybe he understood me; possibly he was just not hungry enough to eat me--whatever his reasons, he turned and waded across the creek, up an embankment, and into a bear tunnel, where he disappeared. What a close call! I suddenly felt quite sick, and it took me several moments to recover before I continued down the stream, pointing my tripod in front of me in the hopes that my luck would hold.

Early that evening, while watching Fish Creek, I caught sight of a young black bear emerging from the bushes. He was probably quite young and looked to weigh only about 100 pounds (45 kilograms). He had likely been chased away by his mother within the last few months. He was still learning how to survive on his own, which became all too clear when he went down to the water and began to chase salmon. After a few unsuccessful attempts, he settled for one of the dead chum salmon Lying along the shoreline.

As the small bear was eating his aged salmon, he was disturbed by a noise to his rear. A large boar came out of the woods. This black bear weighed close to 300 pounds (135 kilograms), and is one of the largest I've ever seen--and he clearly did not appreciate the small bear helping himself to what he viewed as his property. Without hesitation, the small bear hopped across Fish Creek and darted into the woods. The boar followed for a few minutes, but then turned back to the creek and started to fish.

It did not take long for the boar to plunge his head into the water and emerge with a large chum salmon clenched in his jaws.

The bear was so close that I could have touched him-although I did not feel tempted. His beady brown eyes were on me, as water trickled off his fur and the salmon occasionally twitched between his teeth. My heart skipped a beat as the bear looked me over for a very long moment, then turned around and, with the fish still in his mouth, made his way to the other side of Fish Creek.

When the bear reached the opposite shoreline, he placed the salmon down, held it between his paws, then started to eat. Within a few minutes, most of the fish was gone, and only the head and tail remained. Bears in the Fish Creek area will eat the top portion of a salmon head, the egg sacks, and the salmons body. The tail and the face of the salmon are usually discarded, even by the hungriest of bears. In fact, their taste in fish is similar to my own, although I like to clean and cook it first.

Having finished off his first salmon, the black bear returned to the creek and caught a second one. This bear was hungry, and the fish soon vanished. While he was eating, no other bears came near, and they were wise to avoid him. Nothing was going to come between him and his salmon. If another bear had strayed into the area, he would not have lingered; the larger a bear, the more dominant and territorial he is--and this was one big and tough looking adversary. I certainly would not want to quarrel with him.

Below: "Mothers at the bottom of the tree. You come any closer she will take care of you".

This was turning out to be an excellent day for getting photos, and the big bear cooperated by striking many fine poses. But he was not my only model. In the distance, I caught sight of a light-colored cinnamon bear, which wandered over to the shoreline, quickly caught a salmon, then returned to the forest. Luckily for him, the huge boar was too intent on his fishing to notice the interloper. Cinnamon colored black bears, which can be either light or dark, are more commonly found west of the Rockies, so sighting this bear was not that unusual.

I began to hike downstream, and as I walked, there was a scratching sound on a nearby tree. Halfway up was a black bear cub, staring down at me. There is a well-known bear proverb: "Where there is a cub, there is also a mother bear nearby." Therefore, I was cautious and did not make any sudden movements.

After about 10 minutes had passed, the mother bear appeared and walked within about 13 feet (4 meters) of my position before heading towards Fish Creek. With another bear proverb in mind-"Never disturb a mother bear"-I remained still. Within a few moments, the sow had caught a chum salmon and was coming back towards my position. It was at this point that I remembered the most important bear proverb of all: "Do not get eaten by a bear." I shuffled my feet until I was hidden behind a tree. When the mother arrived at the base of the tree where her cub was waiting up in the branches, she dropped the salmon, and uttered a low, grunting noise--the bear equivalent of "Supper is ready."

The cub responded by climbing down. As the proverbs suggest, it is dangerous for a human to be near a mother bear and her cub at any time, but it is an even worse idea to do so when they are eating because bears are extremely protective of their food. I did not want to become part of their meal, nor did I want to disturb them, so I cautiously moved away.

I had walked for only a minute in the direction of the stream when I noticed some bushes rustling on the opposite shore. Directly across from me, yet another black bear came out of the bushes and walked down to the water. This bear was an unusual colour-coal black, except for his legs, which were brown. I later learned this was a very well known bear, recognized locally as Brown Pants.

I slowly sat down in an attempt not to disturb Brown Pants, who was standing right in front of me, but he was utterly disinterested in my presence. There were fish to catch, and his gaze was fixed on the stream. Suddenly, he jumped forward, causing water to splash in every direction, and emerged with a salmon. After eating his snack, Brown Pants continued walking upstream, looking for a main course, but he wasn't having much luck and had to settle for some salmon eggs, which he licked up from the bottom of the stream bed. He was soon out of sight, and this was a disappointment; watching him fish had been quite entertaining. Just after Brown Pants left, another black bear came out of the brush and I got a shot of him licking salmon eggs of the stream bottom.

I then set up my hammock on a nearby tree and tried, unsuccessfully, to go to sleep. Bears were splashing around in the water all night, and it was not particularly restful to contemplate the close proximity of these hungry animals. At the same time, it was a remarkable experience to see the shadows of the bears dance in the moonlight.

Shortly after sunrise a beautiful Red breasted sapsucker was tapping on a tree nearby. He was drilling parallel holes in this live tree,then later the bird will return to feed on the sap and insects that have been attracted by the sap.

At noon the next day, a black bear sow with 2 yearling cubs appeared on the shoreline of the creek. considering she had 2 cubs, this sow was small. But she proved to be an excellent provider. Ignoring the loud splashing of the salmon, the mother bear wandered into the middle of the stream, while the cubs sat down on the rocky shoreline and watched patiently. With a sudden burst of energy, the sow ran down the centre of the creek, stopped, then plunged her head into the water, pulling out a large chum salmon. Next, she waded out of the stream and led her cubs into the woods. The salmon that had been stirred up by the intruding bear returned to their spawning beds, and within a few moments, the creek was once again calm.

It took the sow and her cubs 5 minutes at most to devour the salmon, after which they returned to the creek. The mother bear made a low grunting sound, and the cubs obediently sat down. After a few moments of intense focus on the water, she jumped into the creek, causing a commotion among the salmon. Indeed, the splashing mounted a panicked frenzy. But the sow was indifferent to the plight of her future dinner, and after several quick, graceful movements, she emerged with another salmon. The second helping firmly gripped between her jaws, she returned to the woods, her family close behind.

About 10 minutes later, they were back. I began to wonder just how hungry these bears were-and whether she would mind catching one of those salmon for me. But I was out of luck: the three bears were headed across the creek. About halfway to the other side, one of the cubs playfully tried to snag a salmon. The young bears attempt was futile, and I could relate to his disappointment.

On the opposite side of the creek, the other cub picked up a dead salmon and shook it between his jaws, imitating the movements of his mother after she had caught a fish. Perhaps this was the secret to successful fishing--imitating someone who knows how. After a few moments, the cub dropped the fish in some bushes, and the family wandered out of sight.

I was pleased at having witnessed this fishing lesson, and my attention quickly turned to the stream. I noticed several pink salmon swimming along with the chum salmon; not only did the local bears have volume, they also had variety. Fish Creek is 40 feet (12 meters) across at the place where I was standing-but it contains hundreds of salmon at spawning time. Every section of the creek was saturated by masses of fish. Even I should be able to catch something amid this abundance, but it was late and I had the excuse of being tired.

That night I heard several bears feeding in the creek. It was another moonlit night, and once again I delighted in the magic of their shadows leaping into the water. I was startled when one bear walked directly beneath my hammock on his way to the creek. He may have smelled me, because he stopped as he passed, then grunted and stood on his hind legs before dropping back down on all fours and making his way towards the creek. It was another very long night.

At dawn the next day, a large boar cautiously made his way along the stream and towards me. But about 60 feet (18 meters) away, he stopped, picked up a dead salmon, then returned to the woods. I had a feeling the bear had not gone very far to have breakfast, so I waited and kept a close eye on the nearby trees. After a period of silence, I said a brief prayer, climbed down from my tree, and walked along the shoreline.

This was turning out to be an unusually productive bear-sighting expedition. I had gone only a short distance when I spotted a grizzly sow with a seven-month-old cub, standing on the shore of the creek. This sow was unusually thin and appeared to be in poor physical condition, and the hump on her shoulders was extremely prominent, further indication that she was not eating well or was sick. The bear also seemed very nervous, yet another sign of illness or poor nutrition. Realizing this, I stood very still. The two bears approached me, but as they sensed my presence, they quickly moved away and into the woods.

Three days later, I spotted the infamous bear known to the locals as Big Ears. The name fit. This grizzly had enormous ears and a big grizzly grin. He looked like a clown, but in fact he was just a thin young grizzly that had recently been left on his own and who would have to learn how to catch fish much more adeptly if he expected to gain any stature in his community.

Now that the bear was closer, his features didn't seem quite so odd. Besides, who was I to take issue with his appearance? I probably seemed just as peculiar looking to him. Big Ears grinned at me, then started to chew on a dead salmon that was lying between us. Occasionally, he would smile and watch me, and during those moments I wondered what he was thinking. Once, I even thought I heard him laugh. After a few moments, Big Ears walked away and began to eat some blueberries that were growing on a nearby hillside.

That night, I set up my tent near Fish Creek. It was after midnight when I woke up and realized that a bear was just outside my tent. I remained motionless, and after a few moments of silence, I checked outside--there was the shadow of a large bear, moving away. As always, I felt a little nervous to see such an ominous sight, but what could I do? I returned to my sleeping bag and loudly discussed my genuine love of all forest creatures. This tactic normally puts every living thing in the vicinity to sleep, including myself. It didn't fail this time. The next morning, I woke unharmed--the ideal way to start a day.

My backpack, however, had fared much more poorly, because the bear had climbed the tree where I had hung it. He must have been a very clever bear, because he somehow untied a rope that I had strung between two trees. He must also have been fussy, because all he ate was a single chocolate bar.

With my backpack only a wee bit lighter, I continued hiking. The odor of dead salmon was extremely strong along the shoreline, and several bald eagles flew overhead, searching for snacks. Some of the birds had dark feathers on their heads, which indicated that they were less than 4 years old; when eagles reach 4 years of age, the feathers on their heads molt out white. After taking pictures of the birds, I noticed two grizzlies walking down the nearby hill-side. When they reached the creek both stopped to sniff the dead salmon along the shoreline.

Bear with a meal of Salmon

These grizzlies were not very interested in the aged carcasses and instead went out into the water, where they began to catch live salmon. Unlike me, the grizzlies both caught a fish on every try, their movements were lightening fast.

The bears would rush forward and dive into the water. When their heads reappeared, a fish would be dangling below each bears nostrils. Next, the bear would adjust the flapping fish with its paws to get a better grip, and with a sudden crunch of the bears teeth the fish would go limp. After carrying the salmon to shore, the bear would quickly devour his catch.

Their fishing experience was paying off in the form of a huge feast. The abilities of these grizzlies, and their large size, reinforced the notion that some bears could catch and eat more than 10 salmon a day.

One of the two grizzlies was a sow, who fished in a crisscross pattern that eventually brought her in my direction. When she was about 20 feet (6 meters) away, she noticed me, and must have been startled at my intrusive presence, because she immediately lowered her head and started towards me. The gap between us was quickly closing, but the sow continued to charge, with the bristles of her furry back sticking straight up. I was not sure what this meant, but it was probably not a good sign.

When he reached 10 feet (3 meters) from where I was standing, the grizzly stopped and stared at me. I did not move, except to talk to her in as calm a voice as I could muster. "Don't come any closer, I don't want to hurt you," I said. "Just leave me alone, and I won't bother you." I repeated this nonsense three times--as if I were any match for a grizzly bear. Luckily the bear returned to the creek, where she was soon feasting on salmon again.

I retreated for a quick change of pants, and, with my clothes dry and my pride wounded, I continued to watch the 2 bears. The sow was having extremely good luck at catching salmon, and this seemed to bother the boar. He watched her catch a fish, then he walked over and tried to steal it. The two grizzlies gripped the fish in their teeth, and soon a tug of war broke out. This apparently did nothing to resolve the dispute, because the bears soon forgot all about the fish and began wrestling each other. The match was terrific, especially when the contenders stood on their hind legs, trying to box each other with their front paws. The bout lasted for five or so minutes and ended in a draw. Soon the two nutty grizzlies settled down and waded back into the creek.

After a brief rest, both grizzlies stood up on their hind legs again and stared upstream. They must have been disturbed by something, because they suddenly dropped down on all fours and darted across the creek and into the woods. About ten minutes passed, and then a large cinnamon black bear emerged, grabbed one of the dead salmon and returned to the woods.

"My teeth are longer than yours". "But mine are sharper".

70

A while later, the same bear returned, and this time I spotted a cub at her side. This sow was being cautious with her foraging, in order to protect the cub from other bears that might be in the same area. The 2 wrestling grizzlies had probably smelled her coming and decided to avoid a confrontation. The cinnamon bear grabbed another fish, then she and her cub disappeared into the bushes.

The next day, I was standing on a rock beside the creek when the same 2 grizzlies came out of the woods behind me. The sow walked to within 10 feet (3 meters) of my position, then stopped and stared in my direction.

I began to talk to the bear in a low voice: "Don't come any closer, just leave me alone." The other bear, a boar, closed in to about 13 feet (4 meters) away from me, but he was obviously unconcerned about my presence, because he stood on his hind legs and began to eat some berries off a tall bush. Within a few moments, both grizzlies had left my side and gone fishing in front of me. The bears were easily catching fish with even more ease than the day before. Many of the salmon are now very weak and close to death.

These bears were unique among those I saw during my visit. Every day, for the rest of that week, they would return to the same fishing spot. There, late in the afternoon, they would begin a ritual. After helping themselves to several salmon from the stream, they wrestled for a while, becoming more and more playful until they were gently batting at each other with light, delicate flicks of their paws.

Caught Between a Grizzly And Her Cubs

The dawn of this particular day was especially beautiful. I was deep in the Salmon River valley, and the sun was already erasing the shadows on the hill-sides and it would soon reach this part of the valley. I do not usually carry a watch in the woods, because the last thing anyone wants in an area such as this is to be on any sort of schedule. I can guess from the suns position that it is morning and this is all I need to know.

It is time for my usual breakfast. There is still dew on the morning grass which is evidence that my estimate of the time is correct. As I crawl out of my sleeping bag, the cool morning temperatures cause me to move a little faster in order to create some body heat. The wilderness has no thermostat to turn on, instead you are at the mercy of the clouds. A few warm clothes, however, permit you to stay one step ahead of cool mornings such as this.

One of the great luxuries of this wilderness area is crystal-clear mountain water. The walk to the nearest stream is a short one, but I need to start moving if I am ever to overcome this morning chill. The stream, like many in this area, originates from one of the mountains above me. Although I can't spot any snow on the peaks, I can see a small waterfall within the shadows of the hill-side which means there will be lots of water at my destination. The sun is continuing it's daily conquest of this valley, but some areas such as the mountainside towering above me will remain dim until mid-afternoon. It remains hidden by the adjacent peaks.

The enormous height of these hills can put things into an immediate perspective. Indeed, one cannot help but admire the grandness of it all. Perhaps, this is one of the reasons I have always loved the wilderness. Where else can a person think so well? Each day I seem to have a running conversation with myself. This is not something I have experienced outside of a setting such as this. When a person is trapped among the concrete and the pavement of a city you cannot help but be distracted. But here, the problems of the city do not seem to exist. My mental journey is broken as I rub up against a wet bush. Hiking in wet clothes is not enjoyable but if this is all that can go wrong this morning, then I consider myself lucky.

The air is still today. There is rarely a breeze in this valley early in the day, and this adds to the serenity of this area. Even the sound of the approaching waterfall does not take away from the peacefulness of this area, but instead, adds to it.

I always wash my face in the stream. This to be one of the lost arts. I suspect I played an integral role in misplacing it. Although the goal is a rather simple one--not to drown or get wet in a puddle such as this--it is nevertheless illusive. Wobbly rocks and a lack of balance frequently undermine my efforts.

The shock of the ice cold water on my left sneaker and foot indicate I have failed yet again to master the art. This is the sort of wilderness comedy that surrounds me when I am in the woods. Nature always seems to get the last and usually the first laugh. Nevertheless, the shock of the chilly water on my face eliminates any remaining urge to go back to sleep. So I am at least partially successful.

Few things are more distracting than a sneaker that squeaks when you walk, but this is the price that I must pay for my lack of balance this morning. The key to overcoming this annoyance is to focus on the beauty of this valley. Although it is not a National Park, it should be.

After arriving at my campsite, I enjoyed a small morning feast, and then began the short hike toward the local bear hot spot. I consider Fish Creek to be paradise for anyone that

"Just get out of my way".

enjoys watching bears. Usually the creek is full of spawning salmon through the months of July, August and early September. Bears love to eat salmon and this is the primary meal for the bears in this area. Consequently, Fish Creek offers a great banquet capable of satisfying the appetite of any nearby bear.

I have encountered as many as 11 bears in a single day chasing the fish of this shallow creek. It is the only place that I know of where both black bears and grizzlies can be found catching fish within a short distance of each other. This combination is rare because normally black bears will leave an area where there are grizzlies.

The key to hiking where bears live is to move cautiously. This is the golden rule for survival in bear country. Today, I am violating this basic principle. My movements are faster than they should be, because I am so anxious to see the bears.

The winding trail I am on is narrow, and there are tall trees along both sides. My sneaker is no longer making any noise but there are several puddles that make this hike an obstacle course.

I could see recent bear tracks along the muddy path, but this morning I was not giving them the attention they deserved. The prints should have been an alarm for even the most inexperienced hiker, so I have no excuse for not slowing down. I guess I took the warning for granted, because I see signs such as these constantly.

I occasionally rub up against the thick undergrowth of the forest and the dew is transferred to my jacket. Directly in front of me a large chocolate colored grizzly was moving fast towards me.

I talked loudly, "I'm here. I'm here." The bear put his head up, but kept coming my way.

Two arms length away from me, the bear moved off the trail to my right. All I could see now were the bushes moving. I stood my ground for 10 minutes, and during this time I criticized myself for being so careless. I should have been singing while hiking. This would scare anything. With this bear moving at a fast pace I was sure he was chased by another bear at the creek. I got my wits together, if I had any, then continued on. In the distance, I can detect the faint sounds of running water. It is the familiar sound of Fish Creek. After a sudden turn on the trail, I heard the sound that every hiker dreads: "Whoo, whoo, whoo."

It sounded like a human blowing air out of their mouth, but it was instead the unmistakable sound of an unhappy bear. My suspicion was confirmed. I looked to my right and there was a grizzly coming directly towards me.

My immediate instinct was to turn and run as fast as possible in the opposite direction. However, I knew this would lead me into bigger trouble. Running will only excite an oncoming bear, and this bear was plenty excited already. Moreover, I knew that I could not outrun a bear."Whoo, whoo, whoo," came the ominous sound one more time.

Now the bear was only about two arm lengths away, with its head down. This grizzly had a visible hump protruding from it's shoulder, and the bears small bright eyes were staring directly at me. The bear was in a defensive posture, but if I made the wrong move, I knew this defensive mode could shift to offense quickly.

I was frozen. This is the real problem with encountering a bear in the wilderness. You want to deal rationally with the situation, but your body refuses to move. Panic is the first thing that must be dealt with. Even though I have been in similar situations before, close calls always bring back the same initial feelings of terror. After a few seconds, I began to regain some self-control.

I put my left hand up and said, "It's okay, It's okay. It's just me. I will back up slowly and leave." This is a strategy that has always worked for me. I'm not sure if the bears understand me, or whether they just think I'm crazy for talking to them, but it seems to consistently get me out of trouble. I repeated the message, and began to slowly back up. The bear continued to watch me closely.

Within seconds, I realized the true extent of the problem. Several low grunting noises indicated that I was backing up right into the fryer. This could be trouble. I turned my head to see how bad it was. It was bad. I had been backing up towards 3 bear cubs. Two of the cubs were standing about 13 feet (four meters) away, and the other one was sitting beside them. This explained many things, especially why this sow grizzly bear was so close and concerned with my presence. I was intruding upon her space, and threatening her family. I was not sure if I could talk myself out of this predicament, but I had to do something. The riskiest position I could ever be in was this--standing between a large mother bear and her cubs.

On the other side, the sow continued to watch me closely. She was motionless, and appeared to be waiting for me to make a move.

I turned sideways facing the cubs and said, "Get out of my way, get out of my way". "Get out of my way." This was not an ingenious response, but it was the best I could do.

The cubs did not listen to this plea. Instead these bears that were over one year old began to slowly approach me. This was turning into a disaster. The cub that was closest to me, threw both paws forward and bluffed a lunging motion in my direction. At the same time, he repeated the earlier noise and made a low grunting sound. This was an attempt to threaten and scare me. It was working.

I had to do everything right or I would not survive this dangerous situation, but I was not sure what the right thing was. The sweat is now dripping off my nose, and once again my thinking power came to a halt. My only escape is a small bear trail to my left. If I could only make my legs work, this would be a possible escape route. Finally, my legs started to work. They were shaky, but as long as I was moving I didn't care.

I slowly backed up to the escape route, and while continuing to face the bears, took small steps away from them. As I did this, the sow made a sound by blowing air out between her lips, "Shoo."

Oh, Oh. This was not over yet. All three cubs reacted to the mother bears command and they immediately got behind her. All 4 bears began to follow me. I turned my back toward the animals and tried to maintain a normal walking pace which was no easy task. I occasionally would look behind me to see how close the sow was getting. I was now a fair bit ahead of her, but she was still approaching.

When I reached a tall tree, I got ready to climb. It used to be one of the great chestnuts of wilderness wisdom that grizzlies cannot climb trees. I knew better, because on a previous trip to Kodiak Island I witnessed a large grizzly climb a tree; nevertheless, it is still a good idea to climb a tree in order to give the bear room to pass by, and to reinforce the notion that you are not a threat to the bear. It would be just my luck if this was one of those rare situations where a grizzly was willing to come up the tree after me.

I stood at the base of the tree and prepared to ascend. The perspiration was still rolling off my forehead and my shirt collar was wet. I kept watching for the bear, but all I could see were bushes shaking back and forth a short distance away. A moment later, the sows dark face emerged from the shrubs. Her body remained hidden by the bushes so that her face was framed. I suspect the cubs are with her, but their smaller bodies are probably cloaked by the thick greenery.

The sow remained motionless for a moment and she just stared at me. I stood there as well, and met her gaze. Finally, she glanced to her left and then casually moved off the trail and headed towards Fish Creek which was now within sight. She stood on her hind legs, put her nose in the air, and then looked the area over to see if there were any other threats in the area. Then she got down, and all I could see were the bushes shaking so she moved away from me.

I kept saying to myself, "Your lucky, but foolish. Never be so reckless again." I knew, however, that my excitement would probably get the better of me in the future, and I could count on getting into the same predicament again, despite the tongue lashing I was giving myself.

I remained standing at the bottom of the tree, with my eyes scanning the area. Time and space are both important elements of a bear charge. First you need to give the bear space, and then you need to give the grizzly time to leave the area. No one wants to get a bear upset for a second time within a short period. A bear that gets mad a second time may not be as merciful as they had been during the first encounter, and a real charge instead of a bluff may occur. I kept this wisdom in mind and did not venture from the tree for nearly an hour.

The after effects of this nearly fatal encounter made my legs wobbly and I felt extremely weak. Eventually, my strength came back, and I slowly walked in a route that formed a half-circle of the area in order to avoid the bear family. The bushes were high, and I did not want to bump into my friend again. I took particular care to avoid those spots close to the creek where the bear might be.

The underbrush was very thick, and I created a lot of noise while I was moving. This was good. Noise will typically give a bear advance warning that a threat is approaching and they will frequently leave the area before the threat arrives. This is the reason bear bells are popular with hikers. Because I photograph and study bears, I do not wear them, although I might reconsider after what happened on this day.

Next, I stumbled upon a hole in the ground located in a shady area. This cavity was probably where the sow and her family had rested earlier in the day. The hole was 3.5 feet (1 meter) deep and 10 feet (3 meters) wide. I wondered if perhaps the sow dug this miniature grave for me after our close encounter. This gave me a creepy sensation.

It took me more than two hours to circle the area where the sow and cubs were. I finally managed to make it to the trail that led to my campsite. The entire valley was now lit up by the sun, but I could not admire the beauty of the valley because the incident was still rolling through my mind. I have been charged several times, but this is one of the few close calls I have had with a mother bear. If I had been injured it would not have been the bears fault.

Rufus hummingbird.

Hoss Jumps on a Boar Grizzly

There were quite a few Dolly Varden Trout in the creek. Like the salmon some of these trout migrate to sea and when they come back to the fresh water they are silvery in colour. Dolly Varden trout resemble Brook Trout with red spots, no dark markings and are slender. Their main food are fish eggs and small fish. The biggest one I have seen in Fish Creek was about 15 inches (38 centimeters) long. Dolly Varden Trout living in lakes can weight up to 20 pounds (9 kilograms). Besides Dolly Varden Trout and bears the spawning Salmon attract many different kinds of birds.

A rufous hummingbird flew to a tree and while still flying, but in a stationary position, poked his/her beak into a very small hole that a woodpecker had made. She was getting some sap as she went to every hole in the tree. Another hummingbird came flying by but the intruder wasn't allowed to stay as the first hummingbird drove him off by flying directly at the bird that had just arrived. Air moving through it's feathers produces a humming sound. These hummingbird get to be 3.5 inches (9 centimeters) long and are green, white and rusty brown in colour.

I looked down the creek and there were 2 people wading up the centre of the stream. I knew right away these were employees of the Alaska Fish and Wildlife and they were counting the Salmon. It was Kathleen Wendt and a working companion. Both had a shotgun hanging from their shoulders.

Their feet were causing quite a commotion along the stream bed. I noticed the 2 small dippers scurrying toward the shore, apparently fearful that some predator was making all the noise. When Kathleen spotted me a big smile came to her face. I am used to having people laugh at me with my ancient gear and being continually shabby, but Kathleen's smile was genuine. The sort you expect to receive from a friend you have not seen in a long time. Kathleen appeared to be the same cheerful happy person I had seen the year before. Her arrival coincided with a break in the weather, the dismal overcast shifted into sunshine. This was a shotgun-toting woman who had a deep love for animals. The weapons were required for their jobs and they were rarely used.

"Hello Keith, you haven't been killed by a grizzly yet. I'm happy too see. "

"Maybe someday soon," I replied.

Kathleen gave me a big hug, then she introduced me to one of her new working partner, Andy Piston. He was very quiet as Kathleen and I spouted on and on.

"I saw a bear last month that weighed 1000 pounds."

"Oh yes, well last week I was chased up a tree by a 900 pound Kodiak."

"You should have seen the 700 pound black bear standing on it's head, I came across in the Spring."

On and on it went.

Andy, who was in his early twenties, just listened and smiled, undoubtedly impressed by my strong demeanor and my "overwhelming" intelligence, or something else. Probably something else. Kathleen told me that the salmon run was very poor this year because every fourth year there is a small run of salmon and this was year number four. This means that the number of chum salmon spawning in the creek will continue to be low for the rest of this season.

Kathleen said, "This year there's more bears around than ever before."

I was surprised to hear this because there were so few salmon in the creek, however this information was coming from Kathleen who was a very reliable source, so I knew it was true. This was her fifth year of working at Fish Creek for the Alaska Fish and Wildlife Department; consequently Kathleen has had countless experiences with both Black Bears and Grizzlies. Indeed, this is the only woman that I have ever met who has logged as many bear encounters as I have had. Now she is at the point of talking to the bears, and the ones she knows best she has given names. Her favorite bear was Festus who weighed over 600 pounds (270 kilograms). He had an injured hind leg and he walks with a limp. Rumors in Hyder suggest that Festus was shot by a fisherman.

Kathleen said, "I have not seen Festus this year. Let me know if you see him. Come down to the fish trap and spend some time there."

I responded, "I will be down just before dark."

I spent the afternoon hiking along the creek, then watched a great blue heron and a kingfisher in the Blue Lagoon. This pond is a great spot to watch birds and bears. Both black bears and grizzlies swim, play, and dive to the bottom of this lagoon after dead salmon. The light green colour of the water and the mountains in the background gives this pond a beautiful setting.

I decided to head down to Kathleen's summer home. Both large and small grizzly tracks were on the trail. There is a mother bear with cubs in the area. As the roof of their camp appeared the thoughts of bears temporarily left my mind. My friends had themselves quite a set-up. A large canvas tarp was elevated by plywood sheets and this provided protection from the unpredictable weather in this region. Under the tarp cooking facilities and beds were set up. The campsite itself was situated on the side of a knoll overlooking Fish Creek. This area was surrounded by some massive trees. To my pleasant surprise there were plenty of chum salmon in this part of the creek. They were both above and below the fish trap. The fish trap was right in front of their camp. Both this camp and the trap would be dismantled at the end of each season, which will be late October or early November.

Along with Kathleen and Andy I met the other helper, Ardath Grutney. She is in her early 20's and full of energy like Andy. Both had to have plenty of drive to keep up with their boss, Kathleen. For company and companionship, Kathleen bought her two dogs with her. The smallest of the two is called Vauser, part german shepherd and dingo, and is black in colour, weighting less than 40 pounds (18 kilograms). She is 11 years old. The other dog is a big black Newfoundland retriever called Hoss. He would weigh close to 100 pounds (45 kilograms). Hoss is 2 years old.

Kathleen, Andy and Ardath had very little time to spare as their job kept them busy around the clock. Two or three times each day they would put their waders on go to the fish trap to weigh, measure, tag and with a small pair of tweezers remove a single scale from each fish. This scale would reveal such things as the age of the salmon. After this, the fish are released above the trap. One of their weekly tasks involves hiking up and down the creek counting the salmon that have already spawned and died. This would provide information like how many salmon spawned before being eaten by bears. A job requirement is that each employee carry a gun just in case they come upon a dangerous situation. It is not the sort of job that the average person would enjoy, but these three all seemed to have a genuine love for the fish, bears, the outdoors and their work.

Andy told me that one day while he and Ardath were hiking upstream, right behind them appeared a black bear. The adult bear made his way into the stream and moved to within touching distance of Andy. The bear stopped momentarily, then moved to the side of the creek.

As Andy and Ardath continued on up the creek a sow grizzly came charging at them. This big bear stopped the charge a short distance away from where they were standing. Her two yearling cubs came running behind her, then the cubs ran to the side of the stream and wandered into the bushes. The sow stood her ground and made snarling and grunting sounds. Both Andy and Ardath were very nervous, but stood still in the water clutching their guns. The standoff lasted about 20 minutes, then the sow moved into the bushes where her cubs were. The bear family soon disappeared. Andy and Ardath were shook up by these close encounters.

One of Kathleen's most harrowing experiences occurred during the summer of 1993 when she and another lady biologist named Nicky were counting fish along Marx Creek. A four year old boar grizzly charged them. The bear stopped the charge. Kathleen had her 357 magnum ready, then she started singing joy to the world as loud as she could. Nicky joined in. The bear sniffed the ground, then continued staring. The singing and staring went on for more than fifteen minutes. Finally the boar sniffed the ground one more time and started to wander away. Periodically the bear stared back at them. This gave both Nicky and Kathleen a very eerie feeling.

After this scare, Nicky said, "I don't want to count any more fish today."

We all laughed when Kathleen told this story. She could recount tales such as these with ease. One that I could relate to is the strange conversations involving tourists that one inevitably encounters.

A woman once commented to her husband," Oh honey look those fish are swimming."

She said it as though the fish had some other option.

As Kathleen waded out of the water one warm afternoon a woman said, "Excuse me, what time do you let the bears out?"

Almost everyone that travels through bear country has heard comments similar to these. These comments and stories reminded me of an incident that occurred one afternoon when I was sitting alongside Fish Creek and a black bear was feeding on a salmon directly across from me. The gravel road was only a short distance away. Two tourists stopped to look at the bear. I was in the bushes and these two men couldn't see me. Some rocks came flying over my head with one hitting the bear. Immediately the bear ran into the bushes and out of sight. I was mad so I picked up a rock and heaved it at the tourists. One man reacted by saying, "Lets get out of here, that bear is throwing rocks back at us". They quickly drove away.

After telling stories, I headed back to my campsite with a big smile on my face. Everyday I waited by the fish trap patiently. Just before dark a family of red necked grebes made their way up stream. A mother with nine little ones. Grebes are a stocky bird with a heavy bill, long red neck, white throat and dark cap. The mother dove under the water, got an egg then made her way further down stream. With the little ones following, the family of birds was soon out of sight.

Hiking along the stream bed I spotted a Great Blue Heron standing motionless in a shallow area of the creek and staring down into the water. Like a dart, he scooped up a small fish with it's long beak and immediately swallowed it. This bird has a white head with it's underparts dark in colour, a long beak, long neck and very long legs. These birds can get to be 32 inches (90 centimeters) long and with their wings spread out can be more than 60 inches (150 centimeters) wide. Great blue herons fish by walking very slow in shallow waters then they stand still staring down into the water. When a small fish swims by, they spear it on their sharp bills or catch it in a scissor-like grip. They swallow the whole fish head first. This heron was having no luck at spotting fish. The bird flew further upstream to another spot.

On the third sunny day and late in the morning Vauser started barking and at the same time was staring in the woods behind the camp. Hoss joined in on the chorus, but his bark was louder. Both Vauser and Hoss were tied onto a separate rope and could only run 20 feet (6 meters), which they did. I knew bears were nearby as Kathleen said,"Whenever Vauser barks be 100% sure a bear is near-by". Kathleen contained Hoss and took him by the collar and led him inside the camp. By this time Vauser crawled under the camp.

Sure enough, within moments a sow grizzly with three cubs appeared just above the fish trap. The cubs were about 20 months old and all 4 bears were dark brown in colour. By getting a closer view, I could see that one cub was a little bigger than the other two. The sow made quick movements and right away she caught a chum salmon in her jaws. As soon as she reached the shore one cub attempted to eat the salmon, however the sow grabbed the salmon in her jaws and turned her back to the cub. The cub made her way back to the creek and began chasing the fish. Having no luck she stared at her other two siblings that were down stream sharing a salmon. The young bear waded across the creek, then started up the bank towards me. Oh, Oh, I could be in trouble, now I expected the sow to come charging across the stream.

The cub moved close to me, so I backed up making slow move-ments. My camera case was on the ground, and she began chewing on it. The sow was still on the other side of the creek feeding on a salmon. It was quite obvious the sow wasn't too worried about me. Of course I was giving the cub more room by backing up. The cub grabbed the case in her jaws, then took it down the knoll to the side of the creek and began ripping at it with her teeth. The sow started making her way upstream. With the other two cubs running, the cub dropped my case and ran until she got right behind her mother. All four bears continued upstream until they were out of sight. As for my camera case, it was totally demolished, however the contents inside including a lens and two films were okay.

Just as evening shadows started to appear, a very dark brown boar grizzly that was at least 500 pounds (225 kilograms) came out of woods on the other side of the creek. His whole body appeared to be muscle. Right away, he began chasing the salmon in the pool below the trap. At first, his movements were slow and casual, but when he spotted a salmon he lowered his head and made quick precise movements. As the front part of his body disappeared under the water, almost immediately the bears head surfaced with a chum salmon dangling from both sides of his jaw.

This surprised me because where he caught the fish the water was deep. This boar doesn't have to fish only in shallow areas. He carried the salmon in his jaws to a small island, then by holding the fish with his paws the bear began biting and eating it's flesh. It took the grizzly five minutes to completely eat the salmon. All he left was the tail and part of it's head. The bear slowly made his way down-stream.

The days were sunny and unusually warm for this area. I spent most of my time trying to locate the sow and cubs and during this time I saw another boar grizzly along the creek.

One morning while hiking along Salmon River I spotted a very large boar grizzly that would weigh well over 800 pounds (360 kilograms). His head was very large in proportion to the rest of his body. I was close to the bear and he stared directly at me. The boar put his head down close to the ground. This was a warning for me not to come any closer. I cooperated. In a low tone I began humming then started walking sideways and away from the bear. The big boar still had his head low and as I moved he turned and continued to keep his round beady eyes on every movement I made. Finally the bear headed along the bank of the river.

Every night, for more than a week I couldn't help but dream of how the big boar stared at me, but I was very thankful that he gave me the opportunity to dream again, for this grizzly had all the strength, power and speed to do anything he wanted to do to me.

I continued to hike in the area, but never spotted him again. I have found that when some bears find a new territory, if there's a bear or bears already in the area, then usually the new bears will move on.

I was invited to spend the night at Kathleen's camp and gladly accepted, knowing that my experiences during the night with bears would be just as rewarding as my daytime excursions. Once in the camp my thoughts of my youngest son Steven flashed in my mind. One night he showed me a knife he bought at a store. I told him, "Take it to the store and get your money back because you or anybody else can't have any weapons in a house where I live".

He did so and got his money refunded. If he could only see me now. There was a shotgun by each bunk with handguns to spare, Plus flare-guns. I felt like I was in a gun shop. At times, I walk and talk to bears while my only weapon is my voice. No wonder most people scratch their heads when they meet me.

The night began with the three young grizzlies right in front of the camp. At first the bears moved around and they were nice and quiet, however this prompted Hoss and Vauser to bark as loud as they could. Kathleen's voice stopped the barking. The cubs began a wrestling match and along with this their grunting and growling made both dogs get into the act by barking again. I was in heaven, however, for Kathleen, Ardath and Andy this was far from being pleasant as they wanted to get some sleep. During the night another bear came near the camp. An argument broke out between the bears over the best fishing spot. The grunting, groaning and barking started again. This went on continually throughout the night.

As brightness slowly came to the valley there was complete silence. No bears or dogs were making a sound, however nobody had to be awakened. After going outside and seeing no bears I headed upstream.

The bears were so busy keeping us awake all night that I didn't see them. They must have been sleeping all day. As late afternoon shadows appeared I headed back to the fish trap. Just before reaching my destination a shot rang out. This was unusual, so I hurried to the camp. Kathleen and Andy were wading out of the creek backwards. Kathleen was holding a gun in her hand. In front of her a boar grizzly was circling the fish trap and trying to get in it. When they backed up to me Kathleen said,"That wasn't a shot from a gun you heard, it was from this flare gun. I was trying to scare the bear away from the trap."

The bear was still trying to get into the trap so Kathleen shot the flare gun off again. Instead of taking off the bear headed right towards us. We backed up onto the porch. Now Kathleen had her magnum out and she was pointing it directly at the bear.

She said, "I have never shot a bear before but this could be the first time. Get inside."

The bear was still moving towards us. Andy opened the door. Like a streak of lightning, Hoss came flying out between Andy and I and headed for the bear. Kathleen jumped trying to grab Hoss, but she missed and fell to the ground. By this time Hoss had jumped onto the bears rump. The grizzly was heading for the woods and Hoss still had hold of the bears hair on his rump. Both animals quickly disappeared into the dense underbrush.

Kathleen hollered, "No Hoss, No Hoss, No Hoss."

At this time Vauser had been sick and was burying it with her front paws. I felt like getting alongside her and doing the same thing. At Vauser's age, it's a wonder she didn't have a heart attack.

Ardath was the lucky one, because she had the day off and was in town, so she was missing all the commotion.

We all hollered,"Hoss, Hoss, Hoss". It did no good. To ease her tension Kathleen went down to the trap, and began throwing the Salmon out of the trap into the upper part of the creek. I never saw her throwing the salmon so far and so high. I thought for a moment she was playing basketball.

After 45 minutes of continual calling Hoss was still nowhere in sight.

After a moment I said, "Look at that far mountain, there's Hoss still chasing the bear."

My timing for a joke was not too good. I started barking like a dog, "Whoof, Whoof, Whoof".

Andy joined in, and to our surprise Vauser started barking. Three minutes passed, then Hoss appeared on the other side of the creek. With a little persuasion Kathleen finally got hold of his collar. She was delighted to have Hoss back, safe and in one piece.

During the night Hoss was sick three times. This was probably caused by the excitement, or Hoss had bear hair caught in his throat. After this, he settled down and seemed to be okay.

That night I dreamed of the bear coming towards us. This time instead of Kathleen pointing a gun at the bear, she ordered Hoss to chase the bear away. My dream was more realistic as no matter what, I knew she would not want to shoot the bear.

The following afternoon the same boar that caused all the commotion came out of the woods and started fishing. I thought by this time he would be at least two valleys away looking for a quieter, less violent neighborhood. He stood up, and put his front paw on the wooden walkway and looked both ways.

This is when I realized how big this bear is. On his hind legs, this boar grizzly was over 8 feet (2.4 meters) tall. He got down on all fours and began fishing. Within five minutes the boar caught a salmon, took it to the shore and ate it.

Before going into the woods he took a long look towards the camp. He probably wanted to go another round with Hoss.

That evening, I was alone at the camp when the sow and three cubs appeared and started fishing. Hoss was outside, tied to the tree. I went over, held him by the collar and made my way to the door. Hoss spotted the bears and without hesitation he jumped and headed towards them. At this moment I was still holding onto his collar, and he jerked me off my feet and when I hit the ground Hoss began dragging me towards the bears. Hoss finally came to a stop. I got even with Hoss by literally dragging him inside the camp, then I slammed the door in his face.

The bears were still fishing and obviously neither knew or cared anything about the ruckus that was going on. While the sow was feeding on a fish she stood on her hind legs, stared down stream, then got on all fours and ran into the woods. Her cubs followed.

A big boar appeared momentarily, then turned and headed further down the creek. This bear probably got the scent of the sow and cubs. The sow didn't want her cubs near a boar because male grizzlies are known to kill and eat smaller bears. However boars know that sows are very protective towards their young and without provocation will chase or even attack a bear bigger than themselves to protect their cubs. When a boar comes into an area where there's a sow with cubs, a quick exit is not unusual.

By noon the next day I was hiking on the side of the mountain overlooking Salmon River. At this higher elevation, the wind was swaying the trees and the squeaking sounds from the trees reminded me I was not alone. A mature bald eagle flew by. I was hoping to spot bears on the hill-side eating berries, but with the brush being very thick I was making too much noise hiking, so made my way into the valley and back to Fish Creek. Beside the creek I came to a nice grassy spot and from this point I could see up and down the creek for a long distance. While watching and waiting it was not too long before I fell asleep.

A low grunting sound woke me. I was laying down staring up at a cub grizzly looking down at me. My first reaction was to jump up as fast as I could, but I knew this could very well cause an ugly scene and for sure I would be at the ugly end of it. I slowly stood up and the bear momentarily stared, then she turned and made her way back to the sow and another cub. The sows round beady eyes were staring directly at mine and this made me feel uneasy.

Salmon River

Then as if to say in body language, "Oh, just you again", she turned her back to me and headed up the side of the creek.

I had not seen this sow and two cubs before, however it doesn't mean that they have not seen me. I am sure that I see a very small number of bears compared to the number of bears that see me. These two cubs were in their second year also, but are a little bigger than the triplets that the other sow has. As mother grizzlies chase away their cubs when they are two and a half years old, there's going to be at least five single bears in this area next summer.

Swimming in Salmon River

A few days later I was walking along the shore of Salmon River when I spotted an abandoned canoe. Apparently, some adventurers were going down the river, hit a rock and extensively damaged it. I heard from the wardens that everyone managed to survive the ordeal by swimming to safety. I couldn't figure out why anybody would take such a chance for an adventure, but I guess I am the last one who should criticize anyone for taking that sort of risk.

I wanted to see if the canoe could be repaired, so I could take it along the coastline.

Salmon River is a silty glacier river and in some areas it is 80 feet (25 meters) wide. As long as the water didn't go above my knees, I figured the river would be easy to cross. As usual I figured wrong. I put my sneakers on and began wading. The water was so cold it was like putting my legs into a deep-freeze. Anybody with common sense would immediately turn around. Having very little, I continued to cross. When the water reached just below my knees, I figured the faster I moved, the quicker I would reach the other side. Once again, I figured wrong.

One step later, my whole body sank below the surface. Immediately the swift current pushed me downstream. This was not good. I struggled to the surface, and attempted to balance myself by leaning toward the current. All I could see was white water all around me. The current was pushing me all over the place. I bobbed up and down gasping for air as I went.

After only a few minutes in the icy water, my body was numb. A second passed and the swift water pushed me off my feet and I was under again. I took in some water, but continued to struggle until my head was above the surface. Now the water was deep and pushing me faster and faster down the river. Because of the cold, I was having a hard time moving my arms. In front of me the current was pushing the water up about 6 feet (2.2 meters) into the air. I was waiting for a final death blow from what I suspected was a giant boulder causing this wave. The current pushed me, and I felt like I was on a roller coaster. I went under one more time, and I thought this was it. With all my strength, which was very little, I reached for the surface.

It was then that I noticed a branch just in front of me. The problem was that I no longer had the strength to lift my arm, to grab it. Momentarily, the current pushed me by and I watched as my opportunity slipped out of sight.

A second later, a large rock came into sight. The current was pushing me toward it. I believed this rock would be my last chance for survival, so with all my available strength I dog paddled as hard as I could, grabbed hold of the rock and crawled onto it. I tried to get to another rock that was close to the shore, but my legs would not hold me up. I was too weak, so I laid on the rock and began throwing up.

After about 30 minutes in the sun, I crawled onto another rock then made it to shore. I had to climb up a short knoll, but didn't have the strength to make it, so laid down again taking in the sun. After another 20 minutes of resting I finally made it to the top. Once I reached this ledge I had another session of vomiting and resting. The heat from the sun was putting strength back into my body, so I stood up and began walking. Instead of my legs having their normal strength, I was bobbing up and down like a dipper. I eventually managed to make it back to my camp-site, where I crawled into my sleeping bag and soon fell asleep. I would say that my attempted trip across the river was a disaster, but not totally as I am still alive.

When I woke up, I felt as though I was floating on air. My head was clear as though there was nothing inside it. Based on my previous actions, I suspected this feeling was an accurate mental picture. I keep proving my insanity year after year but this adventure was crazy even for me. I had no problems at this point, because I continued to feel like I was walking on a cloud. Everything was pleasant. This was the after effect of my excursion. I felt so good, I wondered whether I should do it again. No, maybe not.

Somehow my mind has to catch up with the rest of my body if I am to survive much longer. The shock of the incident soon wore off and I happily forgot about the canoe, however everybody soon heard about my swimming excursion.

Below: "Does this feel good

Grizzlies Rubbing their Backs on a Pole

Usually there are plenty of leftovers when a bear is finished eating, and this attracts gulls that continuously fly overhead waiting for the bears to finish. Gulls flying above created a constant noise as they circled. The eagles responded to the ruckus by leaving the area

"Do you have to do everything I do".

seeking quieter feeding grounds along the creek. At times, the birds seemed to get on the nerves of the bears.

While two young bears were feeding at the shallow end of a pool, the gulls were getting very close. The more courageous ones landed within a few feet (1 meter) of a bear. The bear waded towards the gulls. The birds flew away, except for one. For some reason, this bird couldn't fly. The bear lunged at the gull. This gull reacted by spreading its wings and facing the bear in a threatening manner. This posture was not what the bear expected. The bear cautiously moved closer until his nose was about 1 foot (.9 meters) from the gull.

Both the gull and the bear stared at each other for a few seconds, then the gull flapped it's wings and began swimming downstream as fast as possible. The bear chased the gull a short distance but soon became disinterested, and returned to the side of the creek.

There were so many juvenile bears running around that it was difficult to tell one from the other. The grizzlies that came to the creek on a regular basis included the triplets, the twins, the sow, and a good sized boar nicknamed Elvis. Elvis got this name because he would periodically lower one side of his lip. The Black Bears, that were in the area on a regular basis included a sow with two 7 month old cubs, a sow with one 7 month old cub, a small boar called brown pants, a large boar about 400 pounds (180 kilograms), two fair sized charcoal bears and a beautiful cinnamon bear. Further downstream there were more bears, but they had their favorite fishing spots.

Occasionally confrontations would occur when one bear would try to take over another bears spot. One afternoon the triplets made their way towards the twins. I thought to myself, "Oh, No. This could be trouble."

When the triplets spotted the twin grizzlies, they stared, then quickly ran out of the creek and into the woods. The twins were a little bigger in size and in this neck of the woods that is what counts. It wasn't too long before each of the twins caught a salmon. After feeding on their catch, they made their way into the bushes. One of the twins stood on his hind legs and began eating some of the pacific-red-elder berries.

Approximately 20 feet (6 meters) from the creek, along the road is a telephone pole with bear hair on it. These hairs were embedded in the pole as high as 6 feet (1.8 meters) from the ground. This was a scratching pole.

Insects and flies burrow into the fur and bite their skin, so once a bear finds a good scratching tree, or pole, to get rid of the itch, they usually return to it on a regular basis. This was the first time that I have seen a telephone pole used by the bears for this purpose. I spent the next few days waiting to see the bears scratching on this pole.

A car stopped alongside me one time and the man inside said, "Is there a bear here"?

I replied, "Not yet, but I'm expecting one."

They pulled over near the pole and started scanning the area. After 15 minutes the gentleman got out of his car, walked over to me and asked, "How long have you been waiting for this bear"?

I responded, "This is my fifth day here."

The man gave me a disgusted look, walked to his car and said to the two ladies that were waiting, "I'm not waiting any longer with this jerk."

Patience is an essential element of successful bear watching. Being slightly crazy also helps in my case.

The following afternoon, the twin grizzlies were in the creek fishing and having good luck. After feeding on a salmon, one bear slowly made her way up to the pole, leaned against it and rubbed her back by swaying back and forth, then she stood on her hind legs and in an up and down motion rubbed her back against the pole.

She then turned, hugged it, and at the same time wiggled her head and neck against the pole. An expression of satisfaction came on her face as she moved her body sideways, scratching her chest. Her sibling made his way over to the other side of the pole and started scratching his body.

The sow made her way to the creek and the other bear reacted by running to her. Both bears soon disappeared into the bushes.

In the Berry Patch with a Grizzly

I made my way up a hill-side where there were plenty of ripe high bush blueberries. A light breeze was blowing from the west and from this point I could see Salmon River in the valley below. A short distance away the bushes were moving. I knew for sure it was a bear, but because of the tall bushes I couldn't tell whether it was a grizzly or black bear. The bear was directly above me. His head appeared and the bear looked directly at me and his ears pointed in my direction. It was a young sow grizzly. After a moment of staring and as if to say, "Not you again".

The bear began eating the berries. She used her front claws to hold the stems sturdy and in place while eating. Along with the berries the bear was taking in a few leaves which she seemed to enjoy. I spent approximately 45 minutes on the hill with her and during this time she ate at least 20 pounds (9 kilograms) of berries.

As the sow made her way up the hill, I backed up and headed into the valley.

Don't Mess with Nancy

During the summer of 1999, I returned to Fish Creek and found that it was a busy time at the sanctuary. Up to 500 tourists a day were visiting. The number of visitors began to dwindle as the middle of September arrived and their were soon less than 50 visitors each day. Buck and Nancy Maynard are two of my friends that are essentially what I would call the bear police. Together they assist the local protection officers by keeping tourists a safe distance from the bears.

They are armed with bear spray and they patrol the areas where there is potential danger to tourists.Buck is a rugged and strong individual and I have no doubt he could wrestle with a bear if he ever wanted to. If Buck ever started losing to a bear then I am sure he would win with Nancy's help. I recall that Buck once said "nobody but nobody will bother bears when Nancy is around, because nobody wants to mess with Nancy". I have always found this statement to be accurate.

One Sunday afternoon in September, Nancy, a friend and I were watching a sow grizzly making her way along a pond near Fish creek that is known as the Blue Lagoon. The sow was coming towards us but was still a fair distance away. There were about 11 tourists standing near us and they were also watching the bear.

The group consisted of typical tourists and most were taking pictures and commenting on how graceful the bear was. However, there were three young men there with their girlfriends. This is always a recipe for trouble. To make matters worse, they were drinking beer.

The grizzly came to within 40 feet (12 meters) and suddenly one of the men who was clearly drunk started yelling at a bear. A person would have to be intoxicated to do such a thing. I walked behind him and adopted by sternest voice and said "Don't yell at that bear." His friend was a tall man and he did not appreciate my advice and he started to swear at me.

I once again remained calm and simply stated "Don't yell at the bear."

The third man was shorter than his friends and he apparently had hearing trouble because he responded to my sage advice by placing his bear can down and yelling "Come here Bear!"

He then proceeded to scream various obscenities while continuing to request a personal visit from the bear. The tall man stood beside me and said "I am going to jump on that camera of yours and then I am going to kill you."

This was a very unusual day at Fish Creek. Suddenly, I noticed three tourists from Germany prepare my defense. They were each carrying a can of bear spray which they started to point in the general direction of the three hooligans. I simply challenged the tall man and said "Try it."

Upon reflection, I probably could have done better in my response. meanwhile, everyone forgot about the bear who was probably laughing from behind some nearby bushes.

The tall man was now furious. He clenched his fist and looked as though he was going to hit me. All of a sudden a large cloud of bear spray emerged from behind me and hit the ground in front of where I was standing. The tall man was silent. The shortest man pulled back, but everyone seemed to be stunned especially me.

The short man then picked up a rock and threw it toward my head. It just missed me. All three men were now cursing. Then the short man came running past me swearing as he went. I could see that he was running toward Nancy. However, just as he was about to grab Nancy by the neck, she pulled the trigger on the bear spray she was holding. The man was now in a cloud of bear spray and he stopped in his tracks. As the cloud settled I could see that the shorter man's face was completely orange and he was silent. He turned around and ran as fast as he could toward what must have been his car.

He arrived at the car and I was not prepared for what happened next. He took off his shirt, then his pants so that all he had left on was a pair of underpants. He then leaned over a large and dirty puddle and started to splash water on to his face. The other two were still yelling and one threatened to get a gun out of his car and kill me. I lifted my bear spray and said "If I see you get anything out of the car then I will spray your entire car."

The man with the orange head suddenly emerged from his puddle and was once again sprinting toward Nancy and he yelled some obscenities and said "I am going to kill you."

However, by now Buck who is a mighty man was standing in front of Nancy and he obviously had enough of this nonsense. Buck said "Stop, Stop, Stop!"

The man with the orange head thought about this and in fact did stop. I then walked up to the orange man "If you touch her then I will spray you with this."

I held up a full can of bear spray. He turned his orange head away from me and ran down into fish creek and started to scoop up water and wash his eyes and head. He was silent. Nancy and her friend went to Hyder to get help. The tall hooligan looked at me, then picked up a boulder and said, "I am going to kill you."

He must have been nervous about getting a dose of bear spray and this appeared to affect his aim. He missed me by a fair distance. He suddenly became apologetic and offered to shake hands. I suspected this may have been another tactic and I told him to get his orange friend and get out of the area. His comrades were not apologetic and only left after yelling more obscenities. I could see that as the short man sat down in the car he still had an orange glow that I often wonder if he was ever able to remove.

I heard that once they arrived in Hyder they were told to leave town by a group of men who had heard what had happened. They still did not get the message and they bought a large amount of tobacco at a local store. An official with a shotgun arrived with a local man and they escorted the men to the border where they had to give up their tobacco. They were later charged with uttering threats and harassing a bear. The desperados learned something that I have always known and that is that you should never mess with Nancy.

"Hey Buck, Nancy, wait for me".

'um, yum, yum".

"Are you checkin' ME out?"

Above - "You promised me that we would go down to the creek this morning and scare som[e] tourists. I'm not waiting any longer".

Below - "I stomped the fire out. I'll see you at the creek".

Whales surfacing

Whales fishing

"Enough of this, lets wrestle".

Above - "Come on let me in".

Below - "Okay, you win. Let me up". "No".

Two Spirit Bears

White Black Bears

"Stay close to me, that bear is dangerous".

Male big horn sheep (rams)

A Mountain Goat.

Male dall sheep (Rams)

Top - I'm sorry mother, don't stay mad at me.

Bottom - Mother Spirit Bear (white bear) with two black cubs (one lying down behind the black cub

Top - Life of a bear is so tough -Y a w n.

Inset -"I'm sorry, but I can't hang around with you anymore. Mother told me to tell you to go to the glacier and get lost".

Bottom - "I chased a woman who had perfume on, now I am totally exhausted".

Fox

Mule Deer

Native
Salmonids

of the Pacific Northwest, the Canadian Southwest & Southeast Alaska

. **Bull Trout** *Salvelinus confluentas* 2. **Dolly Varden** *Salvelinus malma* 3. **Coastal utthroat Trout** *Onchorhynchus clarki*, female 4. male 5. **Mountain Whitefish** *rosopium williamsoni* 6. **Pygmy Whitefish** *Prosopium coulteri* 7. **Rainbow Trout** *nchorhynchus mykiss* 8. Rainbow Trout steelhead form, sea run 9. Rainbow Trout steelead form, spawning male 10. **Pink Salmon** *Onchorhynchus gorbuscha*, sea run 11. pawning female 12. spawning male 13. **Sockeye Salmon** *Oncorhynchus nerka*, sea run 4. spawning female 15. spawning male 16. **Coho Salmon** *Onchorhynchus kisutch*, pawning male 17. sea run 18. spawning female 19. **Chum Salmon** *Oncorhynchus keta*, ea run 20. spawning female 21. spawning male 22. **Chinook** or **King Salmon** *ncorhynchus tshawytscha*, spawning male 23. sea run 24. spawning female.

"My favourite sport is diving".

Top - "I've got you now".

Bottom - Grizzly licking salmon eggs.

Top - A young grizzly catching a chum salmon.

Bottom - "Oh, Oh, now I am going to have to lick up the eggs."

Above - "Eat it all and you will grow to be big and strong!"

Sockeye salmon

Above - "Thanks Mom".

Below - "Wait for me!".

Boar grizzly. Bears prefer to eat the top part of a s
head, the skin and the eggs.

Bears, though usually prefering to wade, are very s
swimmers.

Background - The hump on a grizzly bears shoulder is muscle.

Above - Others birds and animals are grateful for the feast left behind by the bears.

Above - There are sometimes over 500 people a day viewing Fish Creek Wildlife Sanctuary Alaska to see both grizzly bears and black bears fishing for salmon.

Below - "I'm just taking a walk"

ove - "This is my home".

"What are those things following us, mother"?
"I don't know. I see them all the time".

n sure they are following me!".

Grizzly up a tree.

"No, I'm not coming down until you leave".

Areas that I Hiked in Canada Looking for Bears

Jasper National Park

Jasper National Park is in the province of Alberta just north of beautiful Banff National Park. Besides there being both grizzlies and black bears in this park there is an abundance of other wildlife, moose, deer, elk, caribou, sheep, goats, cougars, and bobcats, squirrels and many species of birds.

The Portal Creek trail is one of my favorite areas and it is very close to the town of Jasper. Portal creek is a small stream that

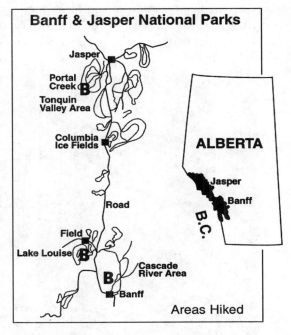

originates high in the mountains and flows downward until it reaches the Athabasca River. Along this stream, there is a hiking trail popular with both hikers and horseback riders.

113

If you hike past the Portal Creek camping area, about 2.5 miles (4 kilometers) up the trail, there awaits some spectacular scenery including rock slides, snow-capped mountains, and alpine meadows. But the best is yet to come. Another 2 miles (3.2 kilometers) along the trail is another campground, located at the beginning of the Tonquin Valley.

If you imagine yourself on a large hill overlooking a sculptured green valley and a winding blue stream, surrounded by mountains, you will have pictured what it is like in the Tonquin Valley. On both sides of the trail leading into the valley are thousands of sub-alpine flowers such as the Indian paintbrush, elephant head flowers, black-eyed susans, columbines, fireweed, violets, thistles and many others.

The green meadows are blanketed with cotton grass, moss campions, white and pink mountain heather,and other flowers. Ground squirrels scurry amongst the rocks, and there are hoary marmots, pikas, weasels, ptarmigans and various types of insects. The meadows attract caribou, grizzly bears, fox, coyotes, wolverines, hawks and owls.

Scenery at the head of Portal Creek.

114

On this particular trip, I had just walked away from several crazy marmots that were playfully fighting with each other in the Tonquin Valley, when I noticed that everything was suddenly still. The single whistle of a marmot broke the silence, then all was quiet again. Looking around nervously, I realized that the cause of this strange lull was an approaching grizzly, light in colour, moving in a criss-cross pattern towards me. The bear was about 300 feet (90 meters) away and coming closer.

Silver-tipped grizzly. "This is fun chasing squirre

The silence was quickly replaced by a chorus of chirping and squeaking, as nervous marmots and squirrels darted for the cover of their burrows. Meanwhile, the bear moved along the hill-side, sniffing at each animal's burrow as he passed it by. One squirrel stuck its head out of its hole and squeaked just as the grizzly moved in the direction of its underground hiding place. The bear raced over to the burrow and began digging wildly, the trapped rodent surely would have been a late afternoon snack had a nearby marmot's whistle not proved enough of a distraction for the squirrel to make its escape. Thwarted, the bear stopped digging and raced across the hill-side, but luckily for the squirrels and marmots it did not return.

Below - The beginning of a rainbow

Darkness was beginning to fall, so I began to hike back to the Portal creek campground. As I was leaving the alpine zone, I spotted a beautiful adult silver-tipped grizzly boar browsing in the grass. He began to dig for roots in much the same way that he would hunt for ground squirrels and marmots--but without the intensity of the search for a live quarry. He reached forward with its front paw to dig, pushing its claws into the ground, then shifted its body to pull away the topsoil. This process easily exposes the roots, which the bear gathered in his claws and ate it on the spot. The Portal Creek area is littered with holes that have been dug by bears searching for roots or burrowing animals.

I continued watching the silver-tipped grizzly tear at the vegetation. He knew I was watching, but he ignored my presence. Casually, he turned his back on me and slowly wandered up an adjacent hill, occasionally digging for more roots. Near the bear, a pine marten slithered its way among the rocks where it captured and devoured a golden-mantled squirrel. All the time I was snapping photographs. There is no lack of subject matter in nature.

I continued to hike in the area for the next 26 days, starting out each day from the head of the trail, journeying to McCarrib Pass and then returning to my campsite. The round trip was about 12 miles (20 kilometers) - an excellent way to get in good physical shape.

At the tail end of my 26 hikes, I finally got lucky, arriving at the meadow just as a sow and her cub were leaving the alpine zone after digging for squirrels. I took a great number of photographs and shot some film footage as well, thankful that my patience had finally paid off.

I was feeling much better about my whole trip, even though I was accompanied on my return trip by what I can only describe as a tropical downpour. I have often wondered if there is a rain cloud that stays in this area waiting for me to arrive. Whatever the explanation, hiking in this area requires determination and patience-and a great raincoat. But I wasn't going to get depressed about the weather. I had taken at least a few good pictures, and after a month of hiking, my legs were as hard as rocks and I felt terrific.

A few weeks later, I returned to Portal Creek for even more punishment. It was sunny the day I arrived and I wondered if maybe I would escape the wrath of the hovering rain cloud. I was just approaching McCarrib Pass when I noticed a grizzly cub.

Realizing that its mother could well be close by, I moved behind a cluster of bushes to get out of sight-but I was too late. The grizzly sow suddenly appeared right next to me and immediately began to close the three-metre gap that separated us. For a moment I panicked and could not remember what to do, but this was no time to lose control, and my rationality quickly returned. I dropped to the ground and covered my head with my hands.

The grizzly approached my prostrate body and systematically sniffed me from head to toe, her sniffs punctuated with occasional grunts. Although my heart was pounding and my adrenaline racing, I managed to find my voice. "I love you", I whispered. "Please don't eat me". Miraculously, the grunting became more and more faint-she was wandering away. After a long moment, I looked up and was relieved to see that the grizzlies were continuing on towards the meadow at a casual pace.

The encounter did not seem to affect either of the bears at all, and they began to graze calmly in the meadow. I, on the other hand, was shaking and my heart continued to pound for some time. The incident had certainly given me a start--and almost an ending. Luckily, I was not hurt, but I was not about to leave the area entirely unscratched. It was raining again. I shook my fist at the sky, smiled, and hiked out.

I returned to the Portal Creek area for another visit the following summer. After two unsuccessful hikes as far as sighting bears was concerned, I began a third trip in. As I neared the high point of McCarrib Pass, I noticed a young grizzly about 30 meters away. This bear was frantically digging for a squirrel, dirt flew in all directions as he got closer to his prey, and the frenzy lasted for about six minutes before he finally sat back on his rump to enjoy his meal. After supper, the grizzly wandered up a hill, sniffing several more holes as he passed, and occasionally stopping to munch the grass.

The next morning, I crawled out of my tent before the sun had peeked out from behind the mountains. This is always a spectacular and beautiful time of the day. I returned to the meadow, hoping to see the same bear as the day before, the lower part of the meadow was empty, but on the hill-side to my right was a sow digging for a squirrel. It was not the same bear, but I was not disappointed in my efforts to get some more mother-and-child photos. A bear cub was standing beside the sow. The cub was on the lookout for anything unusual, and very alert, because he immediately caught sight of my movements. As I stopped fiddling with my camera, the cub stared at me, apparently uncertain what to do.

A few moments later, the sow grizzly poked her head out of the hole and looked my way. Much to my dismay, she left the cub's side and started moving towards me. I began taking pictures, hopeful that the approaching bear would turn back, but she continued advancing, and about 40 feet (12 meters) away from me, started to circle my position.

I remained calm and continued running my movie camera before realizing that I was inadvertently annoying her because of the sound my movie camera was making. The last thing I wanted to do at that point was to get on her bad side, so I stopped the camera, and that seemed to work. The sow turned and went back to the cub, and the two of them walked up a hill-side and left the area. It was beginning to rain-of course!—so I headed out.

Late that night, from my tent I heard grunting, and I reacted like I always do in these situations. I began talking loudly, explaining to any potential furry intruder how much I love all animals and thus deserve to be spared. The sounds stopped. Maybe it was not my voice that scared bears away, as I had always thought, or even my topics of conversation. It occurred to me that there may be another explanation for the hasty departure, at least of that night's visitor. I had my sneakers in the tent, and as anyone who has hiked through mud in sneakers will attest, the smell is terrible. The repulsive smell in the tent is probably the reason that the bear decided not to stick around. I am seriously considering selling my used sneakers as a bear repellent. I could probably make a fortune.

Talking to bears has always been my practice, but on longer trips, I have noticed myself talking to all the animals and even to the flowers. When I get to this point, I realize I have been in the woods too long and it is time to leave. Once, when I actually caught myself saying goodbye to the flowers, I knew it was time for me to reconnect with the human race.

Banff National Park

Banff National Park is also in the province of Alberta, and is just south of Jasper National Park and to the west of the City of Calgary. I headed straight for one of my favorite areas. The trail to the Cascade River is about 3 miles (4.8 kilometers) north of the city of Banff. Besides both black bears and grizzlies , there is also an abundance of other wildlife in the park.

Soon I was hiking along a path parallel to the shoreline of the Cascade River, where I noticed an abundance of soopalie berries. These berries are a delicacy for bears, and a large crop of them, especially ripe ones, can be an indicator of a prime bear area. Soopalie berries are orange and red when ripe, and they grow on both short and tall bushes and are easy for hungry bears to reach.

Because the trail I was on led directly to these berries, I suspected that I had been hiking on a bear trail. That is a path worn into the forest floor by years of regular bear traffic. My suspicions were confirmed when, a few moments later, I noticed animal droppings speckled with whole soopalie berries. Some berries remained intact as they travelled through a bears digestive system. When I saw droppings that contained those berries, I knew a bear could be near-by and that, in addition to soopalie berries, it had recently enjoyed a feast of squirrel, another staple in a bears diet. I recognized the light-brown hairs intermixed with the droppings.

My awareness was now heightened. I continued hiking, with my camera at the ready attached to a strap around my neck. Then I heard the familiar sound I had been anticipating--a deep, guttural "WHOOF". I froze. There it was, emerging from the swaying bushes about 100 feet (30 meters) in front of me--a bear with a hump on his back. This was a grizzly.

The bear was balancing on his hind legs, and from where I stood, he looked like a furry skyscraper. In fact, he was about as tall as I am, but was probably three times my weight. Clearly, this grizzly had all the advantages. A grizzly on his hind legs, glaring into the camera, is quite a spectacular image, although my shaking hands would make it difficult to take any picture.

Nevertheless, I tensed my trembling knees and snapped the shutter, rationalizing that a blurry photo was better than no photo at all.

As I lowered the camera, the grizzly came down off his hind legs and began swaggering toward me. The key to survival in these situations is to remain calm. I had learned this after many close calls. One must always keep in mind that an excited bear is a dangerous bear. Any sudden movements are likely to cause agitation--and this is never a good result. Keeping all this in mind, I slowly and calmly backed up and hiked out of the area.

The next day I was on another bear trail in the same area. I decided to cross a river but this turned out to be an unwise decision, because once I reached the other side I was drenched and cold. As any experienced hiker can confirm, there is nothing worse than hiking in wet clothes, especially wet footwear. Hiking across rivers has been a mistake I have made many times, but I never seem to learn my lesson. So I decided to ignore the dampness and walked along another animal trail that ran parallel to the avalanche area.

I was hardly into my wet journey, when, I was confronted with a mother bear, standing on her hind legs directly in front of me. Behind her stood a large cub. I knew this was a dangerous moment, a sow is very protective of her young and is prepared to chase anything that threatens her family.

My instincts told me this bear did not want to exchange pleasantries with an intruder such as myself--and that, indeed, she might consider making me part of her diet. With these unsettling thoughts in mind, I calmly turned, walked back to the water's edge and once again began the freezing cold journey to the other side and safety. When I got to the centre of the stream, I glanced back to make sure the bears were not pursuing me. By then, the sow and cub were sitting beside the riverbank, watching my ungracious retreat. I will swear they had big smiles on their faces. I gave them an indignant glare and continued across.

The Spatsizi Plateau,
Northern British Columbia -- Hiking With Jim Kahl

Each summer, Jim Kahl and I try to go on at least one hiking trip somewhere in western Canada or Alaska. Jim is one of my oldest friends and he is a lot like me, although he might deny this. He loves nature and he is the sort of person that makes hiking in the woods fun.

In the summer of 1992, we decided to hike to the Spatsizi Plateau, in northern British Columbia. Access to this trail is off Highway 37 in Northern British Columbia on the Alue Lake road. It was dark when we arrived, so we set up our tent about 1 mile (1.6 kilometers) from the head of the trail.

Jim is one of the few people I know who is as excited as I am about hiking in new areas and looking for bears, but on this trip he was feeling nervous because he had a nosebleed--and blood can attract bears. But his desire to observe and photograph bears over-came any anxiety, and we agreed to try to keep a safe distance between ourselves and our furry friends. The next morning, we were raring to go. The hike we had planned was 30 miles (50 kilometers) one way--but Jim and I were both in good shape, so the distance was no deterrent. Jim is a very determined hiker; once he begins hiking, he does not quit until he reaches his destination.

We woke at dawn, packed our gear and began the long hike towards the plateau. The weather had been bad, and quite a few trees had been blown across the path, forcing us to slow our pace considerably in order to negotiate the obstacle course they had cre-ated. I wondered whether my old nemesis, the Portal creek storm cloud, was responsible.

But if we thought the fallen trees were reason to complain, we were in for a real challenge in the form of what appeared to be the world's largest marsh. We found ourselves in the Atlantic Ocean of bogs. We had initially expected to just walk right through it but it proved to go on forever. Jim was as determined as ever, so we made our way along this "trail" for a long distance, sometimes hiking in water up to our knees. It came as no surprise that we fell short of our intended goal for that day, setting up camp after only 18 miles (30 kilometers).

As we pitched the tent, I noticed some blood trickling from Jim's nose, but neither of us was very worried. The hike had been harder than we anticipated, and all we were thinking about was food and a good night's sleep. We were just sitting down to eat when I noticed some bushes moving behind Jim. Not wanting to startle him with this news, I surreptitiously kept an eye on the bushes for any further movement and, as we continued our meal, I kept one hand on a large frying pan--just in case. After supper, we hung our backpacks (with the food inside) on trees a safe distance away from the tent. My pack was about 10 feet (3 meters) above the ground, while Jim's was 6 feet (1.8 meters) higher. When Jim saw my pack, he shook his head worriedly. "It's not high enough," he said. Imagine, questioning the expertise of the bear man! I smiled and assured him that my pack was just fine.

Jim did not seem satisfied with my response, but he was too tired to argue. We crawled into our sleeping bags and were just dozing off when we heard a loud crash. Jim jumped up and stuck his head out of the tent. "My gosh, it's a bear and he has your food," he whispered angrily. "I told you that backpack was not high enough." Well, even so-called experts can be wrong.

We tried to remain calm, but within a few moments, we just had to look outside again. We could hear the grizzly grappling with my backpack. Luckily, the intruder was not near the tree that held Jim's pack, and this was good news. Some of our provisions might consequently survive.

As we watched, the bushes to our right shook. From the sounds of it, the thief was dragging my pack away. Because the bear was apparently leaving, Jim suggested checking to see whether his knapsack was safe. He leapt out of the tent, handed me a can of bear spray, and ordered, "cover me." Then, Jim rushed over to "his" tree and to his delight, his pack was untouched.

Shaken by the incident, Jim and I cautiously returned to the tent and tried to relax. But Jim, unnerved by what had happened, began wondering whether the bear might come back for seconds.

"What should we do?" he demanded.

"Don't worry," I said.

"The bear got my food, so he's not interested in us."

Jim sensed the uncertainty in my voice; he was right. We decided to take turns sleeping; I volunteered to take the first watch, and immediately fell asleep--but not for long. I came awake with a start as Jim shook me, exclaiming, "Wake up! Wake up! How can you sleep with a grizzly roaming around our tent?"

"Jim, don't worry," I answered. "If the bear had wanted to eat us, he would have done it by now."

In retrospect, I don't think this was the reassurance Jim was looking for. In fact, he got more and more agitated, and finally I found out the real reason.

"I have got to go to the bathroom. What am I going to do?" he said.

Evidently, Jim was afraid the bear would get him while he was relieving himself. I sympathized and thought that if you were going to die, that wouldn't be a very glamorous exit.

"Go outside and go to the bathroom," I told Jim. "The bear won't bother you."

Jim gave the bear expert a doubtful look. I'm not sure if Jim believed me, but he did leave the tent, and came back a few minutes later, unharmed. We laughed about our predicament, and then tried to get some sleep. Throughout the night, we heard the bear moving around in the bushes, but the sounds were not all that close by. Still, we were fairly nervous.

The next morning, Jim was very quiet as we got up early to pack our gear and continue along the trail. We still had the food Jim had brought, so we would be all right, and I assured Jim that I would catch some trout to make up for what the bear had taken. As we started hiking, we both kept an eye out for the bear and my missing backpack but saw neither. I was not about to make the possibly fatal mistake of searching for the pack--now the property of that grizzly--and although he said nothing, I was sure Jim was in agreement.

Jim set an extremely fast pace (possibly because there was a bear behind us, or so we thought), and after a few miles of his speed walking, I found that trying to keep up was an impossible task. Besides, my left leg was sore and I began to limp. With Jim's encouragement, I was able to continue, but the trail was in miserable condition, and I began to wonder if anything would go right on this trip.

Jim and I must have been quite a sight as we staggered into the Cold Fish Lake campground. I was hobbling, and Jim was still deal-ing with a bloody nose, and the two of us had been hiking for 16 hours across swamps, over trees, and through mosquitoes the size of pumpkins. But we had made it, and our luck was about to change. We were informed by the camp caretaker that we could rent one of the cabins for six dollars each. The camp had a wood stove, firewood, two beds, and best of all, a roof. Jim and I had hiked to paradise.

The following day, we had completely recovered from our ordeal, and we decided to hike to the plateau, 2.5 miles (4 kilometers) away.

On the way, we stopped frequently to take pictures of the spectacular scenery. The hike was particularly rewarding, and a light rain only added to the beauty that surrounded us. Raindrops illuminated many of the flowers and spider webs, and they glistened as the sun returned. I was glad we were there, despite the earlier mishaps.

Once again, I had to continually urge Jim to slow down because there was no way I could keep up with him. However, Jim had heard this excuse for slowing down on several of our previous trips, so he ignored my plodding pace and continued to hike at his own rate. I decided not to even bother telling him about my difficulties. I had discovered an incredible array of flowers that would be ideal for my slide program--at least, that's the story I would tell Jim.

This was not a complete fiction because the array of flowers I found was spectacular, and it was difficult to pass them by without at least a glance. I must have given them quite the glance, though, because I was only halfway to the plateau when Jim had already arrived. By the time I arrived, he looked upset. Perhaps he was totally disgusted with me.

We soon became absorbed in our surroundings. The view from the plateau was breathtaking, and we could see for several miles in every direction. The plateau itself was unusual since instead of trees, there were enormous green meadows, dotted with large rocks and patches of ice and snow. As well, the flowers on the plateau were in full bloom.

Below - Spatsizi Plateau

Marmots whistled occasionally, and several ptarmigans scurried in front of us, but otherwise this was a very peaceful area. Jim and I had expected to see large animals on the plateau, but we were disappointed. Perhaps it was because the area has a hunting season that only small animals were in evidence. Nevertheless, the plateau was beautiful, and we continued to hike in this area until the sun was about to set then headed back to the camp. On our way down from the plateau, we spotted a moose on a hill-side, but it was too far away to get any good photos. Well, at least we were able to see something bigger than a marmot, even if it was at a distance.

Back at the camp, we struck up a friendly conversation with two other visitors who were also enjoying this spectacular area. They were just finishing their trip and were intending to leave the next day by float plane. After what we had been through, we decided to join them, but we were glad to have made the journey. Although it had not been the smoothest of trips, at least we had seen a bear, though not in ideal circumstances, and experienced some remarkable landscapes.

125

Spirit Bears - Northern British Columbia

Most black bears are charcoal black, brown, or cinnamon-colored, but in northern western British Columbia there lives a very unusual kind of black bear, one that is white. Non-natives call this bear "Kermode," in reference to Francis Kermode, a curator of the British Columbia Museum in the early twentieth century. Another, more romantic name given to this rare animal is a Japanese term that translates as "dream bear."

Native cultures have achieved a special bond with nature, and they have a significant appreciation for these oddly colored bears. In the Tsimshian language of the Indians of northern British Columbia, they are called Moksgm'ol, which means "white bear." Other native peoples refer to them as "ghost bears". The Natives regard the bear as a creature of great spiritual and cultural importance which is a view that I share. Many of the native people I have met consider bears part of our family and refer to them as brothers or sisters. According to Indian legend, a raven created bears, and he made every tenth bear white to remind us of the ice-age glaciers.

I have hiked in several areas looking for spirit bears. These illusive and beautiful animals are difficult to find but have been seen in several spots in British Columbia including north of Terrace, west of Kitwanga, west of Cranberry Junction, and east of Stewart.

I heard several stories that white bears had been seen near Terrace, British Columbia.At that time, I was uncertain whether these "spirit bears," were myth or fact. Consequently, I decided to find out the truth for myself. I began hiking in the Terrace area, on bear trails that led to and from the Skeena and Kitsumakalum Rivers.

The foliage in the area was extremely thick, and my movements created a continual rustling noise as I hiked. As a result, any nearby bears heard me coming, and were long gone by the time I arrived. After sixteen days, the best I could manage was the occasional glimpse of a wide pair of bear buttocks as its owner beat a hasty retreat. This was not exactly an image worthy of the mythical creature I had come to find.

I knew that patience would be my best ally if I were going to properly study and photograph these white bears, so I continued to hike along the Kitsumakalum River, following a bear trail until I was

Mother Spirit Bear (white) with her two black cubs.

able to find a large tree, suitable for a campsite and affording me an excellent view of two nearby meadows. I climbed the tree and set up camp about 15 feet (4.5 meters) above the ground, high enough to allow animals plenty of room to pass underneath.

The shelter I built was made of some tree limbs, and I placed a piece of plastic overhead to act as a makeshift roof. I am always proud of my engineering feats, and this was one of my finest. Unfortunately, nature did not have the same respect for my building abilities, and after a four-hour downpour I was soaking wet.

The next day, I caught sight of a black bear wandering through the meadow. The bear did not stay long, and he was not the colour I had hoped for, but at least the sighting did not consist of a retreating rump. My luck changed a few days later, however, when I spotted a mother bear and two cubs near my camp. The mother bear was creamy white, and the cubs were black with white patches on their chests. After many disappointing days and several wet nights, I had finally found what I had been seeking. I spotted a sow that was definitely a spirit bear. She had probably mated with a pure black bear and created two mixed cubs. It was exciting, but as quickly as they arrived they disappeared.

The following afternoon, my good luck continued. I spotted two more white bears. These bears had seen me before I had seen them, and they were both nervously standing on their hind legs. I stopped moving, and this had a calming effect on the bears. As I watched, they began to wrestle playfully. This activity made for some wonderful photographs. But a few moments later, both of them had vanished into the bushes.

Later that night, I heard a bear underneath my camp high in the tree, but the creaking, rickety structure must have made it nervous, and it quickly ran away. The next morning, not far away, I noticed a white bear travelling with a black bear through the woods. I was careful not to move, but the two bears immediately picked up my scent.

The black bear reacted by quickly running away, while the startled white bear, a sow, ran over to a nearby tree and started climbing, until she reached two sturdy limbs. She rested there a while but never took her eyes off me. I could see that she was uncomfortable with my presence, so I slowly backed away. As soon as I had done this, she climbed down the tree and bolted in the same direction the black bear had gone.

For the next week, I continued to search the area, but I had no luck. By this time, the bears probably knew where I was hanging out, and they wanted nothing to do with a crazy person living in a tree. I decided to pack up my gear and try out a well-padded bear trail that I had seen nearby. In an extremely muddy spot along the trail, I noticed recent bear tracks and droppings. There was also a small stream, where the bears probably came to drink.

I continued to watch the mud hole for several hours. Early in the afternoon, I finally saw a small black bear, which stayed for only a moment before heading back into the woods. For a moment, I thought the bear had caught my scent, but then I realized that he had sensed another bear. The approaching bear was not white, but rather a cream colour, and he looked to be about 170 pounds (75 kilograms) in weight. He saw me immediately, but seemed unconcerned with my presence and continued walking towards the mud hole.

Once there, he waded out to the centre of a puddle that I had not previously noticed, and lay down in the water. After a moment, he began rubbing his neck with his front paw and craning his neck in the air. Then he lowered his head into the water, placing his nose just beneath the surface. This bear must have been extremely warm to lie down in the middle of what was really no more than a mud hole.

After cooling off, the bear left the water and began to eat grass, slowly working his way out of sight as he ate. He did nothing unusual, but I thought it was interesting to see a spirit bear take a bath. Native cultures have always believed that these bears have great power, and I was able to confirm this for myself. Just the sight of this bear, even going through its everyday activities, made me feel good.

Hanna and Tintina Creeks,
Northern British Columbia

Hanna and Tintina creeks flow into Meziadin Lake and they are just south of Meziadin Junction on Highway 37. The streams and rivers of northern British Columbia abound with fish, which usually assures a visitor of bear sightings. When I arrived at Hanna Creek, I was amazed at the numbers of sockeye salmon swimming in the stream. The water looked like a solid mass of fish. Because my visit coincided with the salmon spawning period, the male fish I saw had bright red bodies and light green heads. The female salmon were dark red with green and yellow blotches.

It was a beautiful time of year to be in this area. Winter was coming soon, but for the moment everything was splendid. The mountain peaks were just beginning to change colour, from dark green to bright white, but the fresh snow on the mountainside was unable to overcome the heat of the afternoon sun, and small waterfalls were trickling down the steep mountain cliffs. Soon snow would cover this entire area.

The only distraction from all this splendor was a suffocating smell coming from the shore of Hanna Creek. A number of dead salmon were rotting along the shoreline. The carcasses had attracted several bald eagles, which intermittently fed on the carcasses. I watched the eagles eat their salmon dinner, and tried to take a few pictures. All was peaceful until a young grizzly darted out of the bushes about 150 feet (45 meters) away, then started running towards me. I rose from my crouched position, slipped, and fell to the ground. Nothing seemed to be broken, so I sat upright and watched the bear.

He was still approaching and was now within 30 feet (9 meters). He had slowed from a run to a walk. Nevertheless, I began to mentally prepare my first line of defense--a speech explaining the importance of maintaining good relations between humans and animals. Just as I was about to begin, the bear came to a halt, as if he sensed that he was about to be subjected to something painfully boring. After staring at me for a moment, he turned and jumped into a bear tunnel. Considering I had just arrived at Hanna Creek, this was quite a welcome sight. My heart was still pounding, and I wondered whether such brief bear encounters might have long-term health effects.

With several years knocked off my life, I picked myself up and began walking downstream. Hanna Creek was very shallow, and there were several spots where the backs of the spawning salmon were halfway out of the stream. I continued walking, and every few moments I would glance behind me, just in case the young bear decided to declare war on me. When I arrived at the point where Hanna Creek flows into Meziadin Lake, I noticed that the fish were gathered in extremely large schools. Areas like these would make bears very happy.

I had the use of a canoe, which I thought would be a better way to see more of the area. I paddled on Meziadin Lake to Tintina Creek, and in this case an easy journey-the water was flowing slowly, and there was only a gentle current. After an hour of paddling, I arrived at a well-constructed beaver dam that was making life very difficult for many of the salmon that were trying to get through. They were trying to jump over the dam, but the distance was too great for several of them. The unfortunate ones became entangled in the wood and suffocated. The lifeless fish were brilliant red, and the colour made their twisted bodies beautiful even in death.

After portaging around the beaver dam, I returned to the water and continued paddling. I noticed wolf and grizzly tracks along the shoreline, so I steered towards deeper water. Ten minutes later I saw a cinnamon colored black bear ahead. He approached the stream and stopped right in front of me. I slowed the canoe down, but the bear did not seem to notice me. He was much too intent on the salmon. Suddenly, the bear began to frantically leap and pounce in the stream. The fish fled in every direction, and their red bodies streaked beneath my canoe.

For all his efforts, the cinnamon bear was not catching any fish, and this seemed to agitate him greatly. He ran downstream, stopped, then reversed his direction and headed towards me. Well, I was not to blame if this bear could not fish. I certainly would not blame him for my bad luck as a fisherman. So I stared at the approaching bear and said, "Hold it, hold it." The bear stopped and looked at me, then plunged his head into a shallow area and emerged with a salmon tightly clenched in his teeth.

The cinnamon bear was excited at having caught a fish. It was a feeling I have only rarely experienced, and for a moment I thought he was smiling at me as though he personally knew of my fishing prowess. After a moment, he returned to the bushes.

I was looking forward to more bear sightings, but soon afterward, a steady rain began to fall. I tried to hold out as long as I could, but several days passed, and it was still coming down. I surrendered and returned to civilization.

Kluane National Park, Yukon Territory

Kluane National Park is west of the city of Whitehorse off highway Number 1 in the southwestern part of the Yukon Territory. The Yukon has nature at its finest. There are many areas that remain untouched by the meddling hands of humanity. Visiting the Yukon is a true adventure because it is a wild and enchanting place.

This particular trip to the Yukon began on a sunny July day. The good weather presented an ideal opportunity to hike to the top of Sheep Mountain in Kluane National Park, just west of Kluane Lake and the Alaska Highway. The path consists of a steep, challenging route. During this time, you could hike to Sheep Mountain directly from the highway. Since this trip, however, the park has designated a longer trail that takes you west to Sheep Bullion Plateau. The route has changed because hikers often disturbed the sheep grazing on the mountain.

The first thing that I noticed on this hike was the intermittent chirping and scurrying of Arctic ground squirrels. They were a pleasant distraction from an otherwise monotonous trip which took three hours.

Sheep Mountain is well named, because just as I arrived at the top of the trail, I was greeted by about 50 dall sheep, which were grazing in the green meadows surrounded by rolling hills. Dall sheep are pure white, and since their habitat is covered with snow most of the year, the sheep are well camouflaged.

Most of the sheep in the meadows were ewes with their young. On a distant ridge, the rams were assembled in their own group. I noticed that two of them had broken horns, probably as the result of a mating season battle. Several others appeared to be quite old, because they had fully curled horns.

In spring, grizzlies hunt dall sheep, usually focusing their attention on older animals such as those I saw, since they were probably easier targets.

I began hiking in the direction of Sheep Bullion Plateau which is west of Sheep Mountain. After several hours, I reached the open meadows and soon encountered a grizzly sow with two yearling cubs, feeding on the protein-rich grass that is characteristic of vegetation at high elevations.

I kept a safe distance from the dining bears and watched. The mother bear was being very protective, and she never wandered farther than 30 feet (9 meters) from the cubs. This is common behavior. A sow is particularly careful when cubs that are less than a year old. After getting a few good pictures, I decided it was time to leave.

The next morning, I returned to the same area and at the top of a meadow a fox was slowly moving across a meadow looking for ground squirrels.

I spotted a grizzly boar, or perhaps I should say he spotted me. I say this because he was standing right in front of me, 80 feet (24 meters) away staring right into my eyes when I first spotted him. I looked right back at him, but the bear won the staring contest. Defeated, I slowly turned to my right and began to hike away at a cautious pace. The grizzly continued to stare. When I was about 150 feet (50 meters) from the bear, I breathed a sigh of relief believing that I was now much safer. Indeed, the bear no longer felt threatened, and he wandered away, across a nearby hill. As I walked across the same hill-side, I came upon another fox, and he too watched me closely as I passed.

132

Sheep Bullion Plateau is one of the most beautiful places I have ever visited, and the scenery is breathtaking. There are no trees, and the green alpine meadows extend in every direction, as far as the eye can see. I am uncertain if bears enjoy scenery, but I suspect they do. I am sure that they enjoy the grasses and roots that grow in abundance throughout the plateau; however, their diet is not exclusively vegetarian and this area is also the home of Arctic ground squirrels, moose, and dall sheep. After the main course, the bear must consider dessert. In late summer and fall, the valleys are full of berries, which make a fine sequel to a meal of roots or meat. It is no wonder that bears choose to live in mountainous regions.

Viewing Mount Logan

Mount Logan is in Kluane National Park and I always wanted to see and photograph this mountain. My friends Jim Kahl and Maria Hall decided to hike with me. Maria was born in Sanpurse, Puerto Rico. She then moved to Washington state and met Jim at one of his outdoor education classes. This was her first hiking trip and she was enjoying it. Jim and I were wondering if she could keep up with us, but we soon realized we were having a hard time to keep up with her.

We hiked to the toe of Mount De Coli. Provided the day was nice, we might get a good view of Canada's tallest mountain, Mount Logan from the top of Mount De Coli. Jim put fear into me when he remarked, "This is not a technical challenging mountain to climb". Jim had plenty of experience climbing mountains and I knew he was right but I still wondered. I have wanted to view and photograph Mount Logan for years and I did not want anything to spoil this trip.

We hiked along a stream bed for three hours, and then made our way up a hill and pitched our tents. I was so excited that I decided to go up the mountain right away. I said to Maria and Jim, "I'm going to hike up Mount De Coli right now and I will be back at dark." Jim gave me a curious and nervous smile and said, "go ahead".

Maria said nothing and just smiled. By this time she knew all my marbles were not in the right place. I reached close to a quarter of the way up the mountain and darkness was setting in so I started to head back. When I reached the campsite, Jim smiled and asked me how the view was. I responded, "Good" and would not let this little setback dampen my enthusiasm.

At this point, I suspected Jim was totally fed up with my actions, equipment and appearance. I am not the best organized hiker and my equipment is far from being top gear. I thought it must be driving an organized and well geared hiker such as Jim crazy. Come to think of it most people that hike with me go crazy.

The night was crystal clear and we couldn't help but sit up hoping we might hear some animal sounds, however all was quiet. I was still anxious to go up the mountain so I rose early and went ahead. I believed that the best time to get a clear view of the mountains would be early in the morning before the clouds moved in.

On the way up, four ram dall sheep stood motionless and watched me close as I hiked by. Half way up Mount De Coli, the loose shale rocks made me feel like I was taking one step foreword and two steps back, and at times I was. I reminded myself of Jim's words and that this was not technically difficult. It was still tough and I longed for some new hiking boots or any other new contraption that would make the ascent easier.

After about four hours, I finally reached the top. I was so excited that I had a hard time controlling myself because the far mountains were clear of clouds. All of the mountains to the west were covered with ice and snow. I was looking at the St. Alais mountain range, that consists of the worlds largest concentration of glaciers and ice fields. To the left I could see Mount Vancouver, which has a pointed peak. Far to the right I could see my goal because there in all its glory was majestic Mount Logan.

Mount Logan is one of the most massive mountains in North America as there is a plateau on the mountain that's 10 miles (16 kilometers) long with three conspicuous peaks. On this particular day it was living up to its reputation as a beautiful mountain. Mount Logan is 19,524 feet (5951 meters) tall and is the tallest mountain in Canada. It looks like a gigantic white brick completely covered with ice and snow. The mountain is named after W.E.Logan, founder and long time director of Geological Survey of Canada. On this particular day, the view was overwhelming in all directions but I was in love with Mount Logan.

Late that evening Jim and Maria made their way down the mountain and arrived to where I had my tent set up. They told me that when they reached the top, Mount Logan and the nearby mountains were still in clear view. We were lucky that the weather cooperated with us. Jim looked at my gear, shook his head and smiled.

Polar Bear Country

Although I have been photographing and studying bears for many years, I have always hesitated to travel north, to the Arctic. The pictures of polar bears I had seen were very nice, but I couldn't help noticing all the snow and ice they live in. From my point of view, there is only one thing worse than hiking in wet weather--hiking in cold weather.

I probably would never have set out at all, but one October I stopped thinking rationally and decided to go. I travelled to Thompson, Manitoba, then caught the train that would take me to the frigid north country.

When I got off the train in Churchill, Manitoba, the temperature was below my tolerance level, and there was a cold wind blowing in from Hudson Bay. Churchill was founded in 1700, and is a village with a population of less than one thousand. It is located in northern Manitoba at the mouth of the Churchill River, overlooking Hudson Bay.

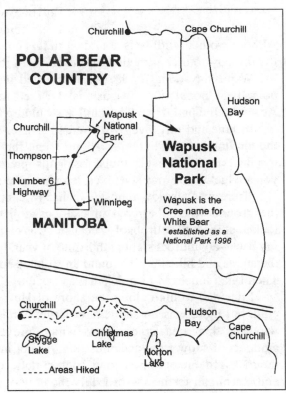

" Don't bug me".

The village consists of a mall, a school, restaurants, a community centre and public library, a hospital, motels, an Eskimo museum, and an airport. There are no highways leading to Churchill. One must arrive by either plane, helicopter, summer canoe, boat, train or walk. The main industry in Churchill is tourism.

Churchill is the polar bear capital of the world, and it isn't unusual for residents to see polar bears in their village. Because of this, I didn't see anyone walking too far from their homes while I was there. Although other wildlife is abundant in this area, polar bears remain the primary tourist attraction in this northern town.

Wapusk National Park was established in 1996 to protect the polar bear population. Wapusk is the cree name for white bear. Access to the park from Churchill is by tundra buggy or helicopter.

In June and July, over two hundred species of birds are found on the tundra around Churchill, among them, the snowy owl, plovers, gyr falcons, ducks, ivory gulls, ross gulls, ptarmigans, and geese. If you are lucky, you may see foxes, lemmings' or a wandering caribou.

There was already almost 3 inches (8 centimeters) of snow on the ground when I arrived in October, and the people I passed looked at me oddly, probably because I was carrying a large pack on my back--an unusual sight at this time of year. I ignored the cold and the stares and hiked until I found an isolated spot to set up my tent. Then I had lunch. My sandwich was frozen.

I decided to hike along the shore of Hudson Bay. It was very cold, but there was no snow, only large, windswept boulders. The wind in this area is constant, which prevents any significant amounts of snow from accumulating, except in a few places beside the rocks. In one of these snowy spots, I noticed fox tracks and several ptarmigan feathers— probably the prey of that fox. I continued walking, and there was an Arctic fox, looking straight at me. He must have assumed I was not a threat, because he ignored me and continued on his way.

The next morning, I crawled out of my tent at daybreak and began to hike along the coastline. By noon, I came to an area where there were recent polar bear tracks. Unfortunately, the snow was starting to fall, and this limited my visibility to less than fifteen meters. I kept repeating to myself, "The weather will not defeat me." I was extremely nervous during this storm; polar bears were difficult to spot during good weather, and they would be impossible to spot in such a storm. I was already beginning to feel defeated.

Thankfully, the storm soon subsided, and I was able to see a bit farther ahead. The snow had stopped just in time; there in front of me was a polar bear, sitting on the trail. I remained motionless, hoping the bear would not see me, and then I realized that its eyes were closed. This bear was sleeping in a sitting position.

I continued to watch, and a few moments later, the bear yawned, rolled onto its side and went back to sleep. A few more minutes passed before it awoke fully, sat up, yawned, then looked sideways and stuck out its tongue.

This polar bear was acting oddly, and I did not think it would be wise to push my luck. The bear had not yet sensed my presence, and I wanted to keep it that way, so I slowly backed away. On the way to my tent, I paused frequently to see if I were being pursued; luckily, I was not.

I decided to travel on one of the tour busses into Wapusk National Park. The locals call these vehicles tundra buggies, and they look like large school busses on big wheels or tracks.

The first hour of the trip we saw ptarmigans and two arctic foxes. We came to an open area and there were polar bears everywhere. The biggest one I estimate was about 800 pounds (360 kilograms) and he gave some people on the bus a scare when he trotted over, stood on his hind legs, and stared in the window. At one time I counted 17 polar bears in the one area. It was remarkable to see so many bears in one small area.

I found this bus trip a little depressing because I was too comfortable. I'm use to being in water, snow or mud up to my rear end. It was a terrific trip in any event and this area was well worth a visit.

Bear Safety Precautions

Roadside Bears

The most likely bear encounter anyone will experience is from behind the windows of a car. It is not uncommon for black bears or grizzlies to travel along roads or in roadside ditches. Some of their favorite foods are grasses and clover. Don't get out of your car.

Bears are strong and if they are within reach they can easily hurt or kill a human. Bears that live near roads become use to seeing vehicles, but once they see a human normally they will run away. If you are too close to a mother with cubs you are automatically a threat. The sow will either charge or take off with her cubs. Do not get out of a car and approach a bear because they may perceive this as a threat.

"Wasn't that funny. Did you see those people scatter when I walked on the road? I felt like having more fun chasing them". "Don't you dare do that. You know a lot of people can't be trusted and they are looking for an excuse to kill us".

Don't feed a bear as they are better off without human food. If someone is hiking where bears live and they have become used to being fed by a human then that bear will probably come after any people it comes across looking for food. Feeding bears can not only get the human in trouble but can often lead to trouble or death for the bear as well.

Taking Pictures

Anyone who enjoys taking pictures of bears must exercise caution. I once saw a tourist with a small box camera get out of his car and run to within 30 feet (9 meters) of a bear, in a foolish attempt to get a close-up shot. Instead of posing, the bear responded by charging the man. I hollered, and this momentarily distracted the bear, allowing the tourist to escape.

If this gentleman had a zoom lens on a camera (not this box camera), he wouldn't have to be this close to get a good picture of this grizzly.

The problem with this tourist's approach was that he had to get close to the bear to obtain his photograph. A much safer way to get a close-up is to use a telephoto lens; in fact, this is an essential piece of equipment for anyone interested in photographing bears--and living long enough to get the pictures developed.

Photographers should also keep in mind that stooping over to take a picture might lead a bear to think you are about to charge him.

This is a threat that bears will respond to, and a bear responding to a threat is not a pretty sight. It cannot be emphasized enough that one must not appear threatening to a bear, and that one must always take pictures from a safe distance. If a bear approaches, back away. Do not worry about objects that are left behind.

In many cases objects left behind stop a bear from coming towards you. A bear usually inspects anything that smells or looks unusual.

Getting Ready For Bear Country.

Usually, a bear that sees or smells a human will avoid contact and leave the area. Problems normally arise from surprise meetings; for example, a hiker may come around a bend and suddenly come face to face with a bear. Trouble can arise from these collisions. Also keep in mind that bears often blend in very well with their surroundings. I have often stared at what I believed was a large rock- and then the rock would get up and begin to move. When hiking, cautiously approach turns in the trail and pay close attention to the details of the landscape.

Preparations for a hiking trip should include several precautions that, if followed, will reduce the likelihood of a bear encounter. I have studied bears in their homes (not in my office) for more than 30 years.

One of the most important steps is not to carry any strong smelling foods into the woods. Avoid meat products, especially bacon or fish; instead, bring freeze-dried or powdered foods. Leave behind all perfumes, scented soaps, lipsticks, make-up, and shaving cream. Anyone with a wound should pay particular attention, and wash it well to remove the smell of blood.

I once sprinkled perfume on some rocks, then climbed a nearby tree and waited to see what would happen. Within two hours, a grizzly sow and her cubs approached the area. The sow stood on her hind legs, sniffed and turned her head in the direction of the rocks. The sow got down on all fours then left the area by moving fast. Darkness set in so I headed back to my tent.

I returned to the rocks the following day to discover the rock had been completely overturned. Bears have an excellent sense of smell, and strong odors make them curious. The last thing a hiker wants is a curious bear coming toward their campsite.

The risk to hikers is greatly reduced if they take a can of bear spray into the woods. Recently, several kinds of bear spray have become popular, and these do repel bears. When the spray is discharged, it is effective against a bear up to 20 feet (6 meters) away. The closer the bear is the more effective the spray is. I wait until the bear is 6 feet (1.8 meters) away. The spray severely irritates the animal's eyes, nose, and skin. The effects of the spray lasts about an hour and does no permanent damage to the bear--if it did, I would not

Bear spray

carry it. I've had to use it four times on grizzlies and it worked all four times. Carrying bear spray when you hike will also provide nervous hikers with psychological comfort; in the event that they do encounter a bear, the impulse to run will be lessened.

Bear bells are another useful piece of equipment, especially in areas with a large bear population. Tied to a backpack during a hike, they will jingle constantly, alerting bears that there is a human nearby and discouraging them from approaching. If bear bells are not available, a tin can with rocks inside will have the same effect. But remember that near a stream, the sounds of rushing water may drown out even the loud ringing of the bells; it is a good idea to sing or talk loudly in this situation so that bears will hear the unwelcome noise and depart. Some hikers carry a small boat horn, which they blow if they see signs of a bear, but under normal circumstances, bear bells are adequate. If you don't like anything noisy like bear bells talk or sing, especially where there are bear signs.

While on the trail, look for signs that may indicate the presence of a bear. The sight or smell of a dead animal should be a signal to circle the area or back away. The sound of croaking ravens, chattering squirrels, or running animals, bear scat,scratches on trees, holes recently dug, fish partly eaten are all signs of bear activity.

A trail with a hump in the centre indicates a path that is frequently used by bears. The pads of bears, paws wear down the trail, leaving a raised area running down the centre. Another indicator is a large number of depleted berry bushes along a trail; bears often feed on berries along the path. Never interrupt a bear that is eating-back away, slowly and calmly.

Indeed, the very presence of a berry patch should prompt caution; after bears eat, they frequently rest nearby. During the berry season, bear droppings may resemble those of cows and contain undigested berries. These berries can be red, orange, blue, or black. Another problem with being in a berry patch is that a bear may think an interloper is trying to steal its food, and this will cause it to become aggressive. Finally, while hiking in an area that has a salmon stream, be on the lookout for overturned rocks, bear tracks, or recently killed salmon--all signs of bear activity.

If children are participating in the hike, be certain that everyone stays close together; a good idea is to encourage them to walk between adults. Even if there are no children, try not to get too far from one another. A rule of thumb is to stay within sight of another member of your party at all times. If hiking alone, inform local officials of your activity so they will know where to find you if you don't come out when you told them you would. If possible, stick to trails that are open enough to allow you to see at least 30 feet (nine meters) ahead. Bears, like humans, prefer trails to struggling through the bush.

It is also important to know bears resting patterns. They are most active just before dark and early in the morning, so try to avoid hiking at these times. The fall of the year is also a very active time for bears and more care is necessary when hiking during this season. Siesta time is usually between eleven in the morning and three in the afternoon. During this period be alert for sleeping bears, and keep a careful eye on the ground while walking in a densely forested area. Bears also tend to be inactive on warm days, when they go looking for shady and cool areas where they can rest. And, of course, the winter months mean hibernation, but some bears sleep more soundly than others, so don't be surprised if you see one in January. The sound of an avalanche or anything close to their den could wake them.

Female Hikers

For women, the menstrual period is not a good time to be hiking in an area where bears live. They have an extremely acute sense of smell and can easily detect blood. If a woman does choose to hike at this time, she should take extra precautions. I once put blood on a piece of cotton and placed it near a bear trail. The cotton was gone the next day and bear scratches and tracks were evident.

Whistling in Bear Country

It is not a good idea to whistle while hiking. Bears may think they are hearing marmots, one of their favorite foods. The call of a marmot is very similar to a human whistle, and the noise will at the very least make a bear curious. I was not always certain that whistling was a bad idea, but after several encounters, I can verify that whistling does not scare a bear away. It has the opposite effect. I have whistled when grizzlies were nearby, and they still approached me. Since an approaching bear is bad news, don't whistle.

Hiking and the Wind

Wind direction is an important factor to consider when travelling in bear country. It is more dangerous to hike downwind of a bear, because the scent will be easier to detect. If the wind is at your back, then heighten your awareness of what is in front of you. If the wind is blowing in your face then you will need to check behind you from time to time.

"No sense in stopping here, this campsites clean".

Camping in Bear Country

Always be careful when selecting a campsite. Provincial or state parks usually have designated camping areas and require that these be used; one cannot simply pitch a tent anywhere along the trail. Although these sites are chosen with safety in mind, some of them are unsafe. Be especially wary of a campground where food-storage and eating areas are located less than 300 feet (ninety meters) from the tenting area. Bears can smell food, even the lingering odors of food, and they will investigate the attractive smells.

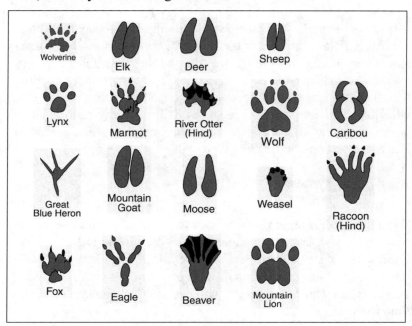

While hiking these are some other animal tracks to look for.

144

Another sign of trouble is an area overrun with squirrels and chipmunks. The presence of many small animals indicates that humans have been feeding them, and they have lingered in hopes of getting more food. The animals themselves-or even the scattered crumbs-may be enough to attract a bear, so avoid campsites with a lot of activity.

If there is an outhouse at the campground, make sure it does not have a strong odor. Unlike human urine, which is repulsive to bears, the smell of human excrement will attract them, and I have even seen them eating it. If there is no outhouse, then walk a considerable distance from the tent to defecate; otherwise the smell may attract a nearby bear.

The condition of the camping area is another important consideration. If there is garbage strewn about, the campground should be avoided. Abandoned garbage strongly attracts bears.

When I go camping, I always check for bear tracks, claw marks on trees, or deep holes left by bears digging for squirrels.

If I see these kinds of signs, I usually sleep in a hammock high above the ground. To keep from falling out of the airborne bed, tie a rope around yourself and attach it to a tree limb. I have spent almost two summers sleeping in a hammock and can report that I was comfortable and safe.

Cooking and Storing Food in Bear Country

When you are camping, it is essential to store and cook food properly. The triangle method is the best way to ensure safe camping-sleeping, eating, and food-storage areas should be kept at least 300 feet (90 meters) apart. This is an excellent way to prevent food odors from drifting towards you as you doze. The last thing a camper wants is a hungry bear in the tent, trying to get at some food. A few cooking precautions are also helpful: remember

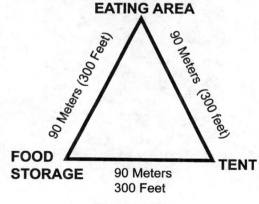

Triangle camping

145

that bears are most active at daybreak and twilight, so plan meals accordingly; and keep in mind that the delicious smell of frying fish or meat is just as appealing to a bear as to a hiker, so use caution.

Ideally, a bear-resistant container should be used to store food, and the safety-conscious officials at parks such as Denali in Alaska provide these to hikers free of charge. Otherwise, seal the food tightly in a plastic bag, making certain there are no openings through which odors might escape.

"Can I go eat what those people are cooking".
"No you can't. Stay here".

Bear proof food canister.

The safest place to keep food is up in the air. Tie a rope between two trees, at least 20 feet (6 meters) above the ground, then attach another rope to the food bag or container and suspend it from the middle of the line. If the food container is properly sealed, a bear that walks under the bag will not detect any odors. If you are camping in an area that has no trees, then seal the food and stash it among some rocks.

It is not uncommon to hear noises outside a tent late at night. If it seems likely that a bear is nearby, make some noise-talk loudly or sing. This noise will usually scare off any nearby animals.

"Whatever they are cooking it smells good. Guess they want me in there too".

Do not get out of the tent to investigate if you believe that a bear has taken your food during the night because this will greatly increase your risk. If a bear has obtained food he will usually rest nearby and protect it, so wait until the morning to check.

Despite the best precautions, it is possible that a bear will get your food anyway. He might climb the tree and knock down your food container, or overturn the rocks that were used as an alpine-zone hiding spot. Under no circumstances try to get your food back; the bear will win any property dispute. And try not to let the theft ruin your trip, just be happy that the food was not stored inside your tent.

I have had my food stolen by bears several times, but I never let it upset me. In one instance, a bear climbed a tree, ripped apart the support line, stole my food and ran off. I could hear it all from my tent, but I did not interrupt the bear. Instead, I made the most of my trip by eating fish and berries for the six days.

This is also an excellent way to lose weight.

I have also been careless, and I always pay for it. On one occasion, I was camping at a government campground. In such places it is easy to assume that no bears will be around-but this is a false assumption, as I soon learned. I had placed my backpack on a picnic table just outside my tent and soon forgot about it. At about midnight, I heard some loud huffing sounds. I sat up and looked outside the tent. Much to my dismay, there was a large bear eating food from my torn pack.

The bear was close enough that I could have reached out and touched him, and for a moment I saw him stare directly at me: just another forgetful camper leaving freebies around. Because the bear was so close, I decided my best option was to cut a hole in the back of the tent and make a cautious retreat. The bear was too interested in my food to bother with me; luckily, I made it to safety. But the incident taught me an important lesson. Never leave food near your tent, no matter how safe you believe it is.

Garbage Disposal in Bear Country

If your food successfully makes it through the night, the next issue to consider is garbage. Food waste attracts bears, so it is important to put all garbage in a plastic bag and seal it. Any combustible food cans that have been emptied should be burned to eliminate odors. If you are in an area where fires are prohibited, then use a plastic bag, sealing the cans tightly inside.

It is not a good idea to bury garbage in the woods, because bears will be able to detect the odors and dig the garbage up. More to the point, they will linger in the area, hoping for seconds. Another good reason not to bury the trash is that a can may harm a bear that digs it up and tries to lick the inside. Garbage buried near a campsite will attract a bear into the area. If you are strong enough to carry food into the woods, surely you are strong enough to carry the garbage back out. The last thing anyone who loves nature wants to encounter is an area destroyed by human garbage.

Dogs in Bear Country

When unleashed dogs are in the woods, they invariably chase bears, which sometimes respond by chasing the terrified dogs right back to their masters. The ensuing-encounter between a maddened bear and a puny human might have tragic results.

Many parks do not allow dogs on back-country trails for this very reason. Check with park officials before going on your trip to see if dogs are allowed in the area. If you must bring a dog, make sure it is on a leash.

Some dogs living in bear country warn their owners of a coming bear by barking, others react by either attacking the bear or running to it's master for protection.

Bear Dens

Hikers who come across a cave, or what looks like a bear den, should leave the area immediately. Hibernating bears have been seen roaming near their dens in winter. They can be awakened by nearby noise, and they may wander in the area, searching for food. Anything that moves in the snow is a potential meal for a bear. If you see a bear in the winter, slowly back away.

Fishing in Bear Country

Bears always have the right of way-especially around a fishing hole. If you see a bear approaching while your fishing, cautiously back away from the area. If a bear should try for a fish being reeled in, cut the line.

Even without bears around, exercise great care in fishing. Make sure to clean your catch more than 300 feet (90 meters) from the tent. After the fish is cleaned, store it in a tightly sealed plastic bag and wash your hands thoroughly. Fish are one of a bear's favorite foods, and if your hands or clothes smell like a fish, a bear may pay you a visit-and he won't be happy with this substitution.

"Give me room to cross over". The bear passed by without incident.

149

Two grizzlies looking at another bear in the creek. This person did everything right by standing still.

Encountering a Bear

On some trips, you may take all the precautions in the world, yet still see a bear. There are many ways to reduce risks. The danger is at its worst if you are within 150 feet (50 meters) of the bear. Sometimes when they get closer a bear may react by making popping sounds with its teeth, or by turning sideways and appearing to ignore you. These are indications that the bear wants you to leave, and you would be wise to comply.

Within 150 feet (50 meters) a bear can see and smell you, and it is important to back away slowly in these cases. If you are on a trail and a bear approaches, cautiously and calmly get off the trail and give the bear plenty of space to pass. Near a lake or a river, wade into the water as far as you can; this will discourage the bear from giving chase. If you encounter a resting bear, back up and leave the area.

The sow was nearby

Never, never, never run away from a bear. Running will only excite the bear, and it will chase whatever is moving. Bears are exceptionally fast runners. When hiking it is pointless to try and out-run a bear as they can outrun any human. Instead of running, stand your ground and use slow movements as you back away; your best defense is to remain as calm as possible.

"Don't worry, I will protect you".

"Move right now. I mean it".

The temptation to run can sometimes overpower clear thinking, and I have seen this happen many times. On one occasion, I was out on the trail with two very experienced hikers. Two large grizzlies suddenly appeared, walking towards us. Jim and Doug turned to run; I grabbed them and told them to remain still.

The bears looked at us for a while, then turned and wandered away. Both men had behaved instinctively, but in this situation it is better to go against any feelings of panic and remain calm. Slow movements help to keep the bear calm, and this will greatly reduce the risk of an attack.

If you encounter a bear cub, realize the danger. A mother bear is very protective of her cubs, (especially cubs that are less than a

"Is this close enough"?

151

year old) and she will react instantly if she hears one of them whine. The sow may not be immediately visible, but rest assured-she is nearby. Again, slowly back away and leave the area.

The worst possible bear encounter for a hiker to experience is to be caught between a sow and her cubs. It is highly likely that the sow will determine your fate. The sight of a charging bear will probably numb your thought processes, but try to remember that running is futile.

Stand your ground; the bear may stop, look you over and then retreat. This will mean that she has only bluffed a charge, and you will have been extremely lucky.

If the bear keeps coming, do not panic. Use bear spray, if you have it, when the bear is within spraying distance which is 20 feet (6 meters).I always wait until the bear is within 6 feet (1.8 meters) away. If you don't have it, drop to the ground and roll up like a ball, protecting your head with your arms. You may be injured but you will probably survive the attack. This is a much better alternative than running. I have had to do this on three occasions, and the charging bear has always reacted by sniffing my body and then leaving. A sow's first priority is to protect her cubs, and she will want to return to them as quickly as possible. The combination of a non-threatening position and a bear's tendency to be repulsed by the smell of human beings, encourages the sow to make a hasty departure.

If a bear does begin to maul you, now is the time to panic. Fight vigorously if your assailant is a black bear; it may react to your behavior by retreating. However, if the bear is a grizzly, your chances of fighting him off are minimal.

Hunting Bears

I do not support bear hunting, but I realize that it does occur and will unfortunately continue. Hunters are the main reason why bears have been exterminated from most of their original homes. Should a bear be injured, he or she will react by becoming aggressive in an attempt to protect itself. I do not blame bears for responding in this way. I believe injuries to hunters are often a result of their own inexperience. If they provoke an attack, they must be prepared to accept the unfortunate consequences.

It's easy to see why humans have exterminated grizzlies from most of their home range throughout the world. I have witnessed both a hatred of bears and the greed some people have toward taking over the bears home range.

People that don't like bears can't stand me. I've had rocks thrown at me, I've been spit on, have been threatened with my life and have been called every imaginable name. No matter what, I will do everything possible to protect the bears and the people in bear country.

"I like tug-of-war".

Hiking In Polar Bear Country

If you should ever happen to find yourself hiking in the Arctic (you never know), there are several warning signs to remember about polar bears. An angry polar bear will blow air out of its nose; if you are nearby, the unusual sound is impossible to miss. Bears trying to acquire a scent will move their head and neck from side to side; if you see these movements, back up and leave the area.

If you encounter a polar bear and are close enough to make a cautious retreat to a car or cabin, then do so-keeping in mind the fact that a bear will notice a moving object more readily than a stationary one. If the polar bear follows, drop your pack, jacket, or any other items that might attract its attention. A polar bear will often stop to check unusual objects; while the bear satisfies its curiosity, you can hopefully make your getaway.

The best way to watch polar bears is from a safe place, such as the tundra tour buses at Churchill, Manitoba.

Report Bear Sightings

When hiking in parks, report bear sightings to park officials so other hikers can take precautions. If one official seems to ignore your volunteer information, try speaking with another.

"Does this taste good".

Most parks have students working in the park for the summer, and most have had very few bear experiences, so make sure your information that you are volunteering is taken seriously. Safety is an important concern for everyone visiting a park.

Living in Bear Country

An obvious precaution for a bear country resident to take is to be careful with garbage. Never leave it out overnight or store it near a residence. If a bear finds garbage once, it will return on a regular basis, and this can lead to trouble. Some municipalities now have bear-proof garbage containers, and these eliminate most of the problems.

For many years, bears freely raided the unprotected garbage at dumps. Many bears would become dependent on this food and turn away from their natural diet; this led to a great many health problems among the bears. Another concern was the encounters between humans and bears in dump areas.

Many communities have since enclosed their dumps with electric fences, making them virtually bear-proof. The bear receives only a slight shock that deters it from returning to the dump area.

The trouble with these electric fences is it has forced the bears into residential areas where they are finding garbage by homes. This has caused bears and humans to be at close range. The old method of having bears at the dump is much safer for residents living in bear country.

Bear Talk

Most of the time, bears are very quiet. Whenever they do make sounds the grunting, popping and squealing is very low. Bear sounds are usually made towards each other.

When disturbed by another bear, animal or human the growling and grunting sounds may be loud. When fighting, bears growl and bellow.

"Whoo,whoo", by a grizzly means for the cubs to get close to her. She may repeat these sounds ordering her cubs to climb a tree. "Huffing" by a sow black bear or sow grizzly will either bring the cubs to her side or send them fleeing.

If a bear is making huff, huff, huff, sounds and is running towards you, the bear is really disturbed about your presence. While hiking in Denali a boar grizzly kept making huffing sounds while he was running towards me. The bear made a U turn and ran back to the berry patch. This was a warning for me not to get any closer to the berry patch. I didn't.

The snapping of jaws means the bear is disturbed. This has happened to me a few times. Every time I backed away and gave the bear more room. When adult bears are mating or playing, grunting will occur but normally they playfully wrestle and lightly strike each other with their paws and make light breathing sounds. Cubs squeal, growl and cry, almost sounding like a human baby at times. This usually occurs when cubs are playing with each other or when the sow plays with her cubs. Body movements and staring are another way bears communicate with other bears and humans.

When a sow bear stands on her hind legs, her cubs usually react by doing the same thing. When this happens the cub runs to mother's side then stands on it's hind legs. The sow standing is a warning that there is danger nearby.

When a bear stares directly at me then puts her nose foreword by just moving her head, a quick charge towards me usually occurs. This is a warning for me to give her more space. When a sow smacks her cub with her paw this means for the cub to pay attention.

Bears are much like humans and they can be moody. During the month of September 1998, I was seeing an adult grizzly every day. The distance between me and the bear was usually about 45 feet (13.5 meters) or more. One day after watching the bear for about 25 minutes she turned her head and looked directly at me, without hesitation she lunged foreword. She stopped, stared momentarily, then moved back to where she had been before and continued to feed on the dead salmon carcasses. This was her way of telling me to keep my distance or perhaps she was just tired of looking at me.

Accidents

Accidents do happen in bear country. Usually, it will involve a situation where someone has not been cautious. People that hunt or walk in wooded areas with powder, perfume, soap, cosmetics, shaving lotion, those with no bear spray, campers sleeping by their food, hikers running away from a bear and all those that are careless with their garbage may find that a bear will react as it would naturally when it encounters unusual smells. I do not think we should fault bears for reacting naturally. They are curious animals who will inspect the source of unusual smells. They can then become excited if they feel threatened and people can get killed. The key is to get people to take precautions. I have made several recommendations above, and I urge everyone to follow them to protect yourselves and the bears. Bears are beautiful animals to watch when it is done safely.

Protecting Bears

I have set out several precautions that people should take when in bear country.

When a human is injured or killed by a bear you need to consider whether the people took the appropriate precautions. I have urged people not to respond by simply blaming the bear.

The Last Resort - Bear Spray Encounters

Having bear spray with me gives me three options to get out of an awkward situation. I first talk to the bear and slowly back away. If the bear continues to come towards me, and when it gets within 10 feet (3 meters) I aggressively yell to let him or her know I'm going to fight, then at 6 feet (1.8 meters) I will spray the bear directly in the face.

Each of the three times I sprayed a grizzly it turned around and ran away or in the opposite direction. On one occasion I am sure I was too hasty as the bear was already half turned just as I used the spray. On two more occasions the aggressive yell stopped the bears from coming further. The last time this happened was at the outlet of Fish Creek when the young grizzly I nicknamed Stalker came after two friends and me. The yelling turned the bear that at this time was within touching distance of us. The following year (2000) Stalker killed a man in Hyder.

I hiked continually looking for bears years before bear spray was invented. At this time I also had three options when bears approached. My first option was to talk cautiously, and to back away giving the bear more room. If the bear continued to get closer I spoke aggressively to let the bear know I was going to fight then if the bear continued to come at me I dropped to the ground and protected my head with my arms.

This worked for me on three occasions. The last time I did this a sow sniffed my body then took off.

On another occasion I got caught between a sow with three cubs. I knew the grizzlies and the bears knew me. This time I slowly backed away and continually kept talking to the sow. The sow and her cubs followed me for about two minutes then she led her family away form me.

Hiking with bear spray now gives me more security in my mind but I will never use it unless its totally necessary, that is, a charge within 6 feet (1.8 meters).

A lot of people have told me that I'm very brave. However I am positive they are being polite, what they mean is "your nuts". Of course I have been told this many times too.

Index